Transformative Action for Sustainable Outcomes

T0299851

This book critically examines sustainability challenges that humankind faces and offers responsible organising as a solution in responding to these challenges.

The text explores how different actors can responsibly organise for transformative action towards sustainable outcomes, as expressed in the United Nations Sustainable Development Goals (SDGs). Responsible refers to a reflexive understanding of how to organise in times of sustainability challenges. Organising refers to activities and practices where different actors take transformative action together. This comprehensive edited collection of short, clear, concise, and compelling chapters brings together scholars in a range of disciplines and blends theoretical perspectives to study humans and social interactions, organisations, nonhumans, and living environments. It offers topical examples from across the world and from organising of companies and other organisations, supply chains, networks, ecosystems, and markets.

The book is written for scholars and students across the social sciences and humanities as well as for practitioners working with the SDGs. It discusses complex issues in an informative and engaging way. It is critical and collaborative. The book serves as an introduction to key themes and perspectives of responsible organising and offers new insights on connections between themes and perspectives.

Maria Sandberg is a postdoctoral researcher at Hanken School of Economics, Finland. Her main research interests are sustainability transitions towards degrowth, sufficiency, and sustainable production-consumption systems.

Janne Tienari is Professor in Management and Organisation at Hanken School of Economics, Finland. His research interests include gender and diversity, feminist theory, strategy work, managing multinational corporations, mergers and acquisitions, and branding, media, and social media.

Routledge Advances in Sociology

For more information about this series, please visit: https://www.routledge.com/Routledge-Advances-in-Sociology/book-series/SE0511

Transformative Action for Sustainable Outcomes
Responsible Organising

**Edited by Maria Sandberg
and Janne Tienari**

Routledge
Taylor & Francis Group

LONDON AND NEW YORK

First published 2022
by Routledge
4 Park Square, Milton Park, Abingdon, Oxon OX14 4RN

and by Routledge
605 Third Avenue, New York, NY 10158

Routledge is an imprint of the Taylor & Francis Group, an informa business

British Library Cataloguing-in-Publication Data
A catalogue record for this book is available from the British Library

Library of Congress Cataloging-in-Publication Data
Names: Sandberg, Maria, 1966– editor. | Tienari, Janne, editor.
Title: Transformative action for sustainable outcomes : responsible organising / edited by Maria Sandberg and Janne Tienari.
Description: Abingdon, Oxon ; New York, NY : Routledge, 2022. |
Series: Routledge advances in sociology |
Includes bibliographical references and index.
Identifiers: LCCN 2021061703 (print) | LCCN 2021061704 (ebook) |
ISBN 9781032135342 (hardback) | ISBN 9781032135366 (paperback) |
ISBN 9781003229728 (ebook)
Subjects: LCSH: Sustainable development–Citizen participation. |
Environmentalism. | Sustainability. | Equality. | Social action.
Classification: LCC HC79.E5 T735188 2022 (print) |
LCC HC79.E5 (ebook) | DDC 304.2–dc23/eng/20220203
LC record available at https://lccn.loc.gov/2021061703
LC ebook record available at https://lccn.loc.gov/2021061704

ISBN: 978-1-032-13534-2 (hbk)
ISBN: 978-1-032-13536-6 (pbk)
ISBN: 978-1-003-22972-8 (ebk)

DOI: 10.4324/9781003229728

Typeset in Times New Roman
by Newgen Publishing UK

Contents

Illustrations

Figure

Table

Contributors

Jana Abikova is a project researcher at the Humanitarian Logistics and Supply Chain Research Institute (HUMLOG Institute) at Hanken School of Economics, Finland, and a lecturer at Prague University of Economics and Business, the Czech Republic. Her research interests are in the fields of human resources in humanitarian logistics, transit migration, refugee crises, criminal aspects of disasters, and human rights violations.

Anna Aminoff is an associate professor in Supply Chain Management and Social Responsibility at Hanken School of Economics, Finland. Her research interests include circular economy, sustainable supply chain management, and procurement. She has initiated and managed research and development projects with research partners, companies, and public funding organisations.

Linda Annala Tesfaye is a postdoctoral researcher at the Centre for Corporate Responsibility at Hanken School of Economics, Finland. Her research focuses on water governance and how technical approaches to water (re)produce socio-economic relations between global South and North, as well as on South-North eduscapes and critical pedagogies.

Frank den Hond is the Ehrnrooth Professor in Management and Organisation at Hanken School of Economics, Finland, and affiliated with Vrije Universiteit, Amsterdam, the Netherlands. He is Co-Editor-in-Chief of *Business Ethics Quarterly* and Editor of the book series *Issues in Business Ethics*. He teaches business ethics and research methods at MSc and PhD levels.

Maria Ehrnström-Fuentes is an assistant professor at the Department of Management and Organisation at Hanken School of Economics, Finland. Her research focuses on the interaction of people, places, and nonhumans in the organising of locally grounded sustainability. She has an extensive record of critically examining the politics of CSR in the interaction between natural resource-based corporations and local as well as Indigenous ways of being on the land.

Martin Fougère is Professor in Management and Politics at Hanken School of Economics, Finland. His main research interests relate to problematising the power effects of business and policy discourses on society. The influential discourses he has critically studied include international business (particularly cross-cultural management), marketing (particularly service management), innovation (particularly social innovation), and sustainable development (particularly corporate social responsibility).

Ashkan Fredström is an affiliated researcher in Entrepreneurship and Management at Hanken School of Economics, Finland. His research interests include creation of new organisations, solutions, and operations in relation to formal and informal institutional establishments.

Meri-Maaria Frig is a postdoctoral researcher at Hanken School of Economics, Finland. Her research focuses on mediated business sustainability communication.

David B. Grant is Professor of Supply Chain Management and Social Responsibility and Dean of Research and Societal Impact at Hanken School of Economics, Finland and Bualuang ASEAN Chair Professor at Thammasat University, Thailand. He is currently working with his co-authors on the third edition of *Sustainable Logistics and Supply Chain Management* for publication in 2022.

Jeff Hearn is Professor Emeritus and Research Director of the GODESS Institute (Gender, Organisation, Diversity, Equality and Social Sustainability) at Hanken School of Economics, Finland, Professor of Sociology, University of Huddersfield, UK, and Senior Professor, Örebro University, Sweden. Recent books include *Engaging Youth in Activism, Research and Pedagogical Praxis*, co-edited with Tamara Shefer, Kopano Ratele, Floretta Boonzaier, 2018; *Unsustainable Institutions of Men*, co-edited with Ernesto Vasquez del Aguila, Marina Hughson, 2019; *Does Knowledge Have a Gender?* co-edited, Örebro UP, 2020; *Age at Work*, with Wendy Parkin, 2021; *Knowledge,*

Power and Young Sexualities, with Tamara Shefer; and *Digital Gender-Sexual Violations*, with Matthew Hall and Ruth Lewis, both forthcoming 2022.

Jonna Heliskoski is a doctoral researcher in Marketing at Hanken School of Economics, Finland. Her research focuses on transformative service ecosystems and social impact marketing.

Tiina Jääskeläinen is a doctoral researcher at Hanken School of Economics, Finland and a project researcher at the Responsive Natural Resources Governance research group at University of Eastern Finland. Her research focuses on epistemic dimensions of recognition in development conflicts in the Sámi homelands and on inclusion and exclusion in natural resource governance and environmental politics.

Neema Komba is a doctoral researcher in Entrepreneurship, Management and Organisation at Hanken School of Economics, Finland. Her research explores the effect of context on entrepreneurial processes.

Jonna Louvrier is an affiliated researcher at Hanken School of Economics, Finland and the founder and CEO of Includia Leadership, a diversity and inclusion consultancy. Her research focuses on the meanings of diversity, difference, and diversity management.

Anna Maaranen is a doctoral researcher in Management and Organisation at Hanken School of Economics, Finland. Her research focuses on the expanding role of social media in contemporary organisations and society.

Eija Meriläinen is a research fellow at University College London, UK, and an affiliated researcher at Hanken School of Economics, Finland. Her work explores critically the roles and power of actors involved in politics of disasters, climate change, and urbanisation.

Charlotta Niemistö is a postdoctoral researcher and Director of the GODESS Institute (Gender, Organisation, Diversity, Equality and Social Sustainability) at Hanken School of Economics, Finland. Her research addresses questions around work/family/care, boundaries between work and non-work, human and social sustainability, organisational well-being, gender relations, age, and generational differences.

Eva Nilsson is a doctoral researcher at Hanken School of Economics, Finland. Her research focuses on practices of, and power related to, corporate responsibility in the Global South.

Kaisa Penttilä is a doctoral researcher at Hanken School of Economics, Finland. She is interested in studying ecosystem level value creation and business models. Her research focuses on managerial sensemaking in transforming business environments in the energy sector.

Visa Penttilä is a postdoctoral researcher at Hanken School of Economics, Finland. His research focuses on the organisational and communicative aspects of corporate social responsibility.

Wojciech D. Piotrowicz is an associate professor in Supply Chain Management and Social Responsibility, and Director of the Humanitarian Logistics and Supply Chain Research Institute (HUMLOG Institute) at Hanken School of Economics, Finland. His research is related to technology and risk in supply chain management, humanitarian logistics, and performance measurement and evaluation. He has considerable experience in international research projects within the public and private sectors.

Pia Polsa is an associate professor in Marketing at Hanken School of Economics, Finland. Her research interests include responsible marketing, consumer vulnerability, poverty, value in cross-sectional settings, and health care service quality.

Maria Sandberg is a postdoctoral researcher at Hanken School of Economics, Finland. Her main research interests are sustainability transitions towards degrowth, sufficiency, and sustainable production-consumption systems.

Beata Segercrantz is a university lecturer in Social Psychology at the Swedish School of Social Science, University of Helsinki and affiliated with Hanken School of Economics, Finland. Her research contributes to critical studies of innovation and care work.

Ya Xi Shen is an assistant professor at Business School, Hunan University, China, and affiliated with Hanken School of Economics, Finland. Her research focuses on individual behaviour, group processes, and organisational practices in multinational corporations, in particular the role of linguistic identity in international business and migrant workplace contexts.

Nikodemus Solitander is a postdoctoral researcher at Centre for Corporate Responsibility at Hanken School of Economics, Finland. They have a keen interest in various forms of neoliberal subjectivity and governmentality.

Karl-Erik Sveiby is Professor Emeritus at Hanken School of Economics, Finland. He is often described as one of the "founding fathers" of Knowledge Management, having pioneered several of the fundamental concepts. His current research interests include a knowledge perspective on responsible organising and sustainability, collective leadership, and critical innovation studies.

Linda Tallberg is an assistant professor in Management and Organisation at Hanken School of Economics, Finland. Her research focuses on human-nonhuman animal relations in business and society with publications on developing an inclusive agenda for nonhuman animals in stakeholder theory, animal dirty work, alternative research methods for animal work, and animal activism in the business school.

Inkeri Tanhua is a doctoral researcher in Management and Organisation at Hanken School of Economics, Finland. Her research focuses on the reasons for occupational and educational gender segregation, considering the intersection of gender and ethnicity.

Yewondwossen Tesfaye is a postdoctoral researcher at Centre for Corporate Responsibility at Hanken School of Economics, Finland. His research focuses on international governance, governmentality, political rationality, discourse, strategies of conduct, subject making, and power relations.

Janne Tienari is Professor in Management and Organisation at Hanken School of Economics, Finland. His research interests include gender and diversity, feminist theory, strategy work, managing multinational corporations, mergers and acquisitions, and branding, media, and social media.

Mikko Vesa is an associate professor in Management and Organisation at Hanken School of Economics, Finland. His research focuses on technological and organisational change, covering topics such as gamification, strategy as practice, and artificial intelligence.

Man Yang is an assistant professor in Management and Organisation at Hanken School of Economics, Finland. Her research interests include ecosystems, sustainable entrepreneurship, and international entrepreneurship.

Ling Eleanor Zhang is a senior lecturer in International Management at Loughborough University London, UK, and affiliated with Hanken

School of Economics, Finland. Her research focuses on expatriates and local employees in both private and public sector organisations from a language, identity, and geopolitical perspective.

Anna Zhuravleva is a doctoral researcher at Hanken School of Economics, Finland. Her research interests include reverse supply chains, sustainability, and non-profit organisations.

Part I

A road map to responsible organising

1 Responsible organising

An introduction

Maria Sandberg and Janne Tienari

Urgent need for change

End poverty in all its forms everywhere. Build resilient infrastructure, promote inclusive and sustainable industrialisation, and foster innovation. Reduce inequality within and among countries. Achieve gender equality and empower all women and girls. Ensure sustainable consumption and production patterns. Take urgent action to combat climate change and its impacts.

These are just some of the goals that the world needs to achieve by the year 2030, as set forth by the United Nations' 2030 Agenda for Sustainable Development. Agenda 2030 is a roadmap for sustainable development, signed by all UN member states. Its central element is the 17 "Sustainable Development Goals" (SDGs), which identify different areas of sustainable development that require our immediate attention (see Box 1.1). The SDGs define sustainable outcomes for both social and environmental sustainability challenges.

The SDGs present formidable challenges for humankind and urgent action is needed in and across societies to reach the goals. This book provides insights into how different actors can organise for transformative action towards sustainable outcomes, as expressed in the SDGs. We propose the concept of "responsible organising" for state-of-the-art thinking on how to tackle sustainability challenges.

Responsible organising

This book critically explores and examines conventional approaches to sustainability and suggests new ways of thinking and organising for sustainable outcomes. The book offers new paths forward that recognise the complexities and connections inherent to sustainability challenges today and in the future.

DOI: 10.4324/9781003229728-2

Box 1.1 The 17 Sustainable Development Goals

The 17 Sustainable Development Goals as defined by the United Nations' Agenda 2030 (https://sdgs.un.org/goals):

SDG 1: No poverty
SDG 2: Zero hunger
SDG 3: Good health and well-being
SDG 4: Quality education
SDG 5: Gender equality
SDG 6: Clean water and sanitation
SDG 7: Affordable and clean energy
SDG 8: Decent work and economic growth
SDG 9: Industry, innovation and infrastructure
SDG 10: Reduced inequalities
SDG 11: Sustainable cities and communities
SDG 12: Responsible consumption and production
SDG 13: Climate action
SDG 14: Life below water
SDG 15: Life on land
SDG 16: Peace, justice and strong institutions
SDG 17: Partnerships for the goals

We propose responsible organising as an umbrella concept for the organisational, socio-ecological, and transnational processes required to tackle sustainability challenges and achieve sustainable outcomes. "Organising" refers to how different actors take action to change and transform organisations, societies, and transnational institutions. It draws attention to activities and practices. "Responsible" refers to a reflexive understanding of how to organise for sustainable outcomes. We believe that it is how sustainability is understood and acted upon that lies at the core of finding solutions to the challenges we are facing.

Responsible organising helps to address a variety of fundamentally important challenges and solutions in organisations, societies, and transnational connections. The book zooms in on practices through which people can tackle and fight sustainability challenges by doing things in new ways, organising for transformative action, and infusing organising with responsibility. Our examples range from individuals, families, and groups to companies and other organisations, networks, ecosystems, supply chains, and markets across the world.

The book offers topical examples of responsible organising for transformative action towards the SDGs from different fields and geographical settings in both the Global South and North to illustrate its key points. The book covers all 17 SDGs. The authors represent 13 nationalities and the geographical scope in their work used as examples is vast, including Australia, Chile, China, Ethiopia, the EU, Finland, Haiti, India, Kenya, Tanzania, and USA.

This edited collection of short, clear, concise, and compelling chapters brings together scholars in a range of disciplines all with a keen interest in studying responsibility, equality, and sustainability. The book is authored by experts in different fields based at, or affiliated with, Hanken School of Economics in Helsinki, Finland. We are not only an international, but a multidisciplinary and interdisciplinary academic community that has established a space for researching, discussing, and fostering action on responsibility, equality, and sustainability. The book draws from research in fields such as corporate responsibility, sustainability science, macromarketing, social marketing, supply chain management, organisation and management theory, decolonial studies, and gender, diversity, inclusion, and intersectionality studies. It blends theoretical perspectives to study humans and social interactions, organisations, as well as nonhumans and living environments. We argue that a boundary-crossing approach is needed to make explicit and tackle questions of responsibility, equality, and sustainability that are complex, interconnected, and often ambiguous and contested.

The book is divided into five parts. The first part (Chapters 1–4) discusses the need for new ways of understanding sustainability challenges. It suggests the need to rethink how we address responsibility, (in)equality, and sustainability in three central ways: rethinking corporate social responsibility (CSR), refocusing the idea of diversity to tackle inequalities, and engaging with the nonhuman world in new ways. The next three parts provide discussions and examples of novel ways to organise in these areas. Table 1.1 gives an overview of the geographical settings and SDGs covered in the chapters in Parts II–IV. The fifth and final part summarises the book's key messages in a single chapter.

Responsibility in a changing world

In Part II, we discuss how (corporate) responsibility can be made useful in organising for transformative action for sustainable outcomes. Conventional approaches to CSR have been argued to lack the ability for transformative action, as argued in Chapter 2. The chapters in Part II suggest a variety of ways to rethink responsibility and provide examples

Table 1.1 Overview of the geographical settings and SDGs covered in the book

Chapter	Geographical setting	SDGs
5	Global	3, 9, 10, 13, 16
6	China, USA	17
7	Finland	16, 17
8	Finland	7, 12, 13, 17
9	Europe	3, 8, 9
10	EU	1, 2, 10, 12, 13
11	Finland, India, Kenya	1, 3, 8, 12, 15, 17
12	Haiti	10, 11
13	Ethiopia, Tanzania	1, 10, 17
14	Global	4, 5, 10
15	Tanzania	4, 5, 8, 10, 12
16	Global North	3, 5, 8, 10
17	Finland	13, 15
18	Ethiopia, India	6, 9, 10
19	Australia, Global	12, 14, 15
20	Chile, Finland	10, 11, 13, 15

of how companies and other organisations can approach responsible organising in new ways to contribute to sustainable outcomes. The chapters discuss the need to recognise changes in the global environment, how to strengthen CSR activities through collaboration with stakeholders, and responsible organising of different parts of the operations of companies and other organisations.

Chapters 5 and 6 provide analyses of the global environment, which lay the foundation for responsible organising. Chapter 5 analyses global risks that need to be recognised when organising for sustainable outcomes. The authors identify interconnected risks that are critical for the sustainability of societies. One such risk is changes in the political landscape. Chapter 6 picks up on this key issue and analyses how the re-emergence of geopolitics is changing the global environment. The authors suggest that the SDGs have potential to be useful for easing geopolitical tensions and opening up dialogue across the world on how to organise for sustainable outcomes globally (SDG 17).

Chapters 7 and 8 provide examples of how companies and other stakeholders can organise in multi-stakeholder initiatives to achieve sustainable outcomes. Chapter 7 gives an example of a cross-sector collaboration that used political action to call for regulation of corporate conduct. The authors argue that organising for political action in such a way can strengthen corporate responsibility by making certain practices mandatory for companies. Chapter 8 shows how energy production

(SDG 7) can he made more sustainable when companies and other actors align their activities to create value for society. The authors argue that such an ecosystem approach to responsibility is necessary for transforming systems of production and consumption (SDG 12).

The final chapters in Part II discuss how to organise the operations of companies and other organisations more responsibly. Chapters 9–11 provide analyses of the responsibility of different parts of organisational operations: organisational innovation, supply chains, and marketing. Chapter 9 shows how fostering innovation (SDG 9) in organisations can have negative consequences on the advancement of other SDGs. The authors argue for the need to better understand the (ir)responsibility of organisational innovation. Chapter 10 analyses the sustainability of supply chains for textile reuse. The authors discuss the role of non-profit organisations in reorganising supply chains in response to new legislation. Finally, Chapter 11 discusses how markets and marketing of organisations can be made more responsible and contribute to achieving sustainable outcomes. The authors argue that there is a need to reverse the logic of markets and marketing.

Challenging inequalities

In Part III, we discuss how to challenge inequalities across the world. A prominent way for companies and other organisations to address inequalities in the last decades has been the focus on diversity and inclusion. Chapter 3 discusses shortcomings of this approach and argues for a need to rethink how we address inequalities and social justice. The chapters in Part III discuss how inequalities are presently addressed and suggest new ways of organising responsibly for equality.

The SDGs include the need to reduce inequalities both *among* and *within* countries (SDG 10). The chapters in Part III address both aspects of organising for equality. Chapters 12 and 13 discuss how to reduce inequalities among countries. The authors critically examine how unequal relations between countries in the Global South and Global North are maintained through current relief, aid, and development practices. Chapter 12 discusses how the organising of humanitarian relief maintains unequal power structures between the countries providing and receiving aid. To address these inequalities, the authors suggest reorganising humanitarian supply chains. Chapter 13 discusses the transformative potential of multi-stakeholder partnerships that aim to end poverty in the Global South (SDG 1). The authors argue that current ways of organising fail to address structural inequalities and discuss how to (re)organise partnerships for transformative action.

Chapters 14–16 address how to reduce inequalities within countries and organisations, among families, and at the level of individuals, with a particular focus on gender equality (SDG 5). While Chapter 14 addresses a global issue, Chapter 15 addresses inequalities in the Global South and Chapter 16 in the Global North. Chapter 14 critically examines how social media algorithms maintain and reinforce inequalities. The authors show how technology that was designed to cherish diversity and equality in practice works against reducing inequalities. Chapters 15 and 16 analyse how systems of inequalities – such as gender, age, social class, and marital status – intersect. Chapter 15 analyses inequalities experienced by women in the Global South. The authors argue for the need to recognise context-dependent intersectional inequalities when organising for equality. Finally, Chapter 16 discusses intersectional inequalities in work and care in the Global North. The authors suggest a need to (re)organise work and care to address gendered and other inequalities in systems of production and reproduction.

Engaging with the nonhuman world

In Part IV, we explore how to include the nonhuman world in discussions of sustainability today and in the future. Chapter 4 argues that new ways of engaging with the nonhuman world are necessary for responsible organising. In this vein the chapters in Part IV challenge conventional thinking about the environment and suggest new ways of engaging with the nonhuman world. The chapters are united in a call for recognising the voices of local communities and marginalised actors. They provide examples from different local contexts of responsible relations with the nonhuman world.

Chapters 17 and 18 question current approaches to engaging with the nonhuman world. Chapter 17 discusses nature-human relations in disaster governance. The authors problematise the nature-human dichotomy and discuss how nature-human relations are constructed in local communities. Chapter 18 discusses our relation to water, analysing how global discourses about "affordable" water (e.g., SDG 6) diffuse in local communities. The authors show how current ways of organising water governance produce inequalities in local communities. The chapter thus illustrates the interconnectivity of sustainability challenges, showing how social inequalities and relations to the nonhuman world are intertwined.

Chapters 19 and 20 discuss new ways of engaging with the nonhuman world. Chapter 19 discusses how to consider nonhuman animals when organising for sustainable outcomes. The authors criticise conventional

approaches to sustainability for excluding nonhuman animals and analyse the potential of market-based accreditation schemes to represent
nonhuman animal voices. Finally, Chapter 20 presents examples from
local, Indigenous communities of engaging with the nonhuman world
in ways that challenge conventional approaches. The authors argue that
recognising and learning from local communities is essential for responsible organising and transformative action for sustainable outcomes.

In all, the chapters in the book present a multitude of ways that
different actors can responsibly organise for transformative action
towards sustainable outcomes. The final chapter of the book, Chapter 21,
brings all these discussions together to suggest ways forward for responsible organising.

2 Corporate social responsibility is useful only when it is *made* useful

Martin Fougère and Nikodemus Solitander

Introduction

This chapter offers a constructive critique of the concept of Corporate Social Responsibility (CSR) and suggests ideas on how to make it more useful. In the early 1990s, CSR became important for business largely as a response to the sustainable development agenda and the heightened regulatory pressure it was associated with (Banerjee, 2008). CSR became institutionalised in big business from the mid-1990s, when large interest groups such as the World Business Council for Sustainable Development (WBCSD) were formed and when corporations such as Nike and Shell were targeted by activists exposing their corporate irresponsibility. These watchdog movements led to reactive PR campaigns that gave birth to new practices, such as CSR reporting (Shamir, 2004). The value of CSR has been argued by its proponents to lie in its ability to tackle a range of sustainable development challenges through voluntary self-regulation, and thereby be "good for society" (WBCSD, 2002).

However, the supposedly positive macro-effects of CSR on the economy, the environment, or society have never been proven, despite a few attempts to do so (CSR Impact Project, 2013). Instead, a great deal of evidence suggests that CSR has mainly been useful for re-legitimising powerful business interests (De Roeck & Delobbe, 2012) in times of widespread corporate critique that could otherwise lead to tighter regulation or even losing their social license to operate. For many critical scholars of CSR, this is what makes the concept problematic: the main positive impact of CSR seems to be on business, not on society (Banerjee, 2008; Fleming & Jones, 2013; Schendler, 2021). Banerjee (2008, p. 59) characterises CSR as "an ideological movement designed to consolidate the power of large corporations."

While we agree with Schendler's (2021) recent observation that CSR, as designed by business on the terms of business, has been at best a

DOI: 10.4324/9781003229728-3

"well-intentioned distraction" and at worst knowingly complicit with the interests of the fossil fuel industry, we argue that CSR *can* be useful. Evidence shows that when it has been useful for nature and society, it is because it was *made* useful as a result of active mobilisation of non-business stakeholders. We argue that in responsible organising for sustainable outcomes, the actors that shape CSR usefully – whether through multi-stakeholder mobilisation in relation to policy initiatives like the United Nations Sustainable Development Goals (SDGs) or through more adversarial types of action – are non-business stakeholders.

The pressure it took to make CSR (more) responsible

The adoption of CSR practices by large companies in the 1990s came as a reaction to pressure from the United Nations, governments, and civil society. Business interest groups first defined CSR as voluntary self-regulation and companies started reporting on CSR as any positive impact they might argue they have on nature and society beyond minimum legal requirements (WBCSD, 2002). The emphasis on voluntariness made it possible for business to reclaim legitimacy by foregrounding all the value they "proactively" create for nature and society, while engaging in aggressive lobbying against regulation by arguing that self-regulation is the most effective way to tackle sustainability challenges.

Voluntary definitions remained dominant until 2010 due to such lobbying efforts, notably in the EU (Shamir, 2010), despite evidence that progressive CSR practices always appeared as responses to stakeholder pressure. It took strong mobilisation of civil society stakeholders and to some extent governments to develop new influential definitions whereby CSR should be understood as the responsibility of companies for their impacts on society. An example of this was the new definition of CSR adopted by the EU Commission in 2011 (EU Commission, 2011). The timing of this mobilisation was facilitated by the 2008 financial crisis, which posed a threat to the social license of business to operate and was the target of relentless critique in the media and by politicians.

In parallel with the development of CSR practices in individual firms, a new institutional form called multi-stakeholder initiatives (MSIs) emerged in the 1990s. These "soft law" arrangements, relying on market regulation and involving certification of sustainable production (Moog et al., 2015), were a result of large business interest groups partnering with large corporate-friendly NGOs – with explicit support from the UN. These MSIs were spearheaded by large buyers of commodities derived from crops that cause rapid land use change, and which are responsible for massive negative externalities in subtropical areas. Prominent examples of crops regulated by MSIs include oil palm and soybean (Schouten et al., 2012). Here too, the design of MSIs as consensus-aiming deliberative efforts served the legitimacy needs of large corporations, while the mobilisation of stakeholders from outside the MSIs have helped in improving the MSIs and making their standards more demanding (Fougère & Solitander, 2020).

Making CSR (more) useful

When developed on the exclusive terms of business, CSR has been shown to be self-serving and useful mainly from the perspective of the legitimacy needs of business. When non-business stakeholders have engaged with CSR, they have at times succeeded in making CSR more useful for society, even if this transformation is often incremental and marginal. If CSR really holds the potential to be useful for society, it is precisely because it opens a possibility for stakeholders to engage with companies' CSR claims through various means, some more of the partnering kind, others explicitly adversarial, and others in between these two positions. We suggest three forms of action for non-business stakeholders to make CSR (more) useful: (1) business-aligned stakeholder actions, (2) agonistic dialogue and regulation, and (3) radical, subversive interventions.

Making CSR useful through business-aligned stakeholder actions

The most obvious type of business-aligned stakeholder action to make CSR useful consists of forming a cross-sector partnership that genuinely attempts to address a significant sustainability challenge. A good illustration of such a partnership is the Carrefour-WWF collaboration to terminate the delivery of plastic shopping bags. This dyadic NGO-business partnership involved one of the largest retailers in the world and absolute market leader in France, and eventually led to France being the first country to prohibit the delivery of plastic bags by the cashiers of supermarkets in 2016. This legislative prohibition later inspired many other countries to follow suit.

A potential example of business-aligned stakeholder action is also the ecosystem approach to responsibility showcased in Chapter 8. Another intriguing example relates to the performative role of CSR researchers and their ideas. Here, belief in the link between Corporate Social Performance (CSP) and Corporate Financial Performance (CFP), which originated in and disseminated through business schools, has become to some extent self-fulfilling through feedback loops, gradually making the CSP-CFP link more of a reality (Martı & Gond, 2018).

Making CSR useful through agonistic dialogue and regulation

Some watchdog organisations have moved from a traditional adversarial approach to a more constructive approach aimed at dialogue while resisting co-optation into partnerships. They make CSR useful for incremental sustainability improvements by scrutinising corporate claims of CSR and seeing to it that companies act upon them properly. The Finnish organisation Finnwatch, discussed in Chapter 7, applies this type of strategy to try and close governance gaps, mostly through improvements to soft law arrangements such as MSIs. They put pressure on the MSI to improve its standards and their enforcement, as in the example of the Roundtable on Sustainable Palm Oil suspending the certification of leading oil palm plantation company IOI soon after a Finnwatch investigation in 2016.

However, non-business stakeholders can also go beyond soft law to influence regulation. As seen in Chapter 7, Finnwatch has taken a core agentic role in transforming human rights due diligence from a matter of voluntary corporate policy to one of national legislation in Finland.

Making CSR useful through radical, subversive interventions

Non-business stakeholders can also take more radical action to make CSR useful. Traditional "blaming and shaming" campaigns can be particularly effective in making companies more socially responsible. This often involves hijacking CSR and marketing and/or advertising tricks through "culture jamming." For example, the Finnish animal rights organisation Oikeutta eläimille (Justice for animals) designed a campaign targeting the largest Finnish retail chain that is also a leader in CSR. The campaign included footage of animal abuse in farms and relied, among other things, on the subvertisement "The biggest cage egg farm in Finland" (see Voima, 2021). As a result of the campaign, the company eventually stopped using eggs produced in battery cages.

Subversion through culture jamming can provide memorable ways of exposing not only cases of corporate irresponsibility but also the limits of CSR, by "taking CSR too seriously" (Fleming & Jones, 2013; Fougère, 2021), demanding the total realisation of CSR claims through subversive interventions. One illustration of this approach is the Yes Men posing as Dow Chemical representatives and claiming, live on BBC World, that Dow will "take full responsibility" for the Bhopal disaster, including a 12 billion dollar compensation package for the victims. Engaging in such "what if" counterfactuals probably cannot right the corporate wrongs – in this case Dow soon claimed that the announcement was a hoax and their share value, after taking a big hit, quickly returned to its prior level. However, the reaction in financial markets made it clear that making the responsible decision in this case – taking responsibility for the negative externalities – does not pay from the financial perspective. It thus contributed to understanding the limits of what a voluntary understanding of CSR can achieve in publicly listed corporations.

Conclusion

CSR on the sole terms of companies will always be an attempt to re-legitimise business as almost usual. In this chapter, we have shown how non-business stakeholders can contribute to making CSR useful for society. However, the change that occurs by making CSR more useful (whether through partnerships or more adversarial approaches) is only one type of change. Transformative initiatives that are developed *despite* or even *against* business and CSR will also be needed when tackling global sustainability challenges.

SDG 17, with its injunction to develop multi-stakeholder partnerships to address these grand challenges, provides opportunities to make CSR useful through business-aligned stakeholder actions but does not make it easier for non-business stakeholders to be agonistic or radical when engaging in dialogue (or conflict) with business (see Chapters 13 and 20). Such a non-critical framing of business-stakeholder relationships will not go far in dealing with wicked problems in ways that do not systematically prioritise business interests – and it can only be self-defeating if we are serious about addressing contemporary capitalism's dismal record in terms of social and planetary boundaries.

References

Banerjee, S. B. (2008). Corporate social responsibility: The good, the bad and the ugly. *Critical Sociology*, 34(1), 51–79, https://doi.org/10.1177/0896920507084623

CSR Impact Project (2013). Impact measurement and performance analysis of CSR. Available at: https://cordis.europa.eu/project/id/244618/reporting

De Roeck, K., & Delobbe, N. (2012). Do environmental CSR initiatives serve organizations' legitimacy in the oil industry? Exploring employees' reactions through organizational identification theory. *Journal of Business Ethics*, 110(4), 397–412, https://doi.org/10.1007/s10551-012-1489-x

EU Commission (2011). A renewed EU strategy 2011-14 for corporate social responsibility. Available at: https://eur-lex.europa.eu/LexUriServ/LexUriServ.do?uri=COM:2011:0681:FIN:en:PDF

Fleming, P., & Jones, M. T. (2013). *The End of Corporate Social Responsibility: Crisis & Critique.* London: Sage. http://dx.doi.org/10.4135/9781446251935

Fougère, M. (2021, online ahead of print). Resignifying corporate responsibility in performative documentaries. *Journal of Management Inquiry.* https://doi.org/10.1177/10564926211005030

Fougère, M., & Solitander, N. (2020). Dissent in consensusland: An agonistic problematization of multi-stakeholder governance. *Journal of Business Ethics*, 164(4), 683–699. https://doi.org/10.1007/s10551-019-04398-z

Marti, E., & Gond, J. P. (2018). When do theories become self-fulfilling? Exploring the boundary conditions of performativity. *Academy of Management Review*, 43(3), 487–508. https://doi.org/10.5465/amr.2016.0071

Moog, S., Spicer, A., & Böhm, S. (2015). The politics of multi-stakeholder initiatives: The crisis of the Forest Stewardship Council. *Journal of Business Ethics*, 128(3), 469–493. https://doi.org/10.1007/s10551-013-2033-3

Schendler, A. (2021). The complicity of corporate sustainability. *Stanford Social Innovation Review*, 7 April 2021. https://doi.org/10.48558/KKJB-K728

Schouten, G., Leroy, P., & Glasbergen, P. (2012). On the deliberative capacity of private multi-stakeholder governance: the roundtables on responsible soy and sustainable palm oil. *Ecological Economics*, 83, 42–50. https://doi.org/10.1016/j.ecolecon.2012.08.007

Shamir, R. (2004). Between self-regulation and the Alien Tort Claims Act: on the contested concept of corporate social responsibility. *Law & Society Review*, 38(4), 635–664. https://doi.org/10.1111/j.0023-9216.2004.00062.x

Shamir, R. (2010). Capitalism, governance, and authority: The case of corporate social responsibility. *Annual Review of Law and Social Science*, 6, 531–553. https://doi.org/10.1146/annurev-lawsocsci-102209-153000

Voima (2021). Vastamainokset. Available at: https://voima.fi/vastamainokset/ (accessed 26 November 2021)

WBCSD (2002). *Walking the Talk: The Business Case for Sustainable Development.* Geneva: World Business Council for Sustainable Development.

3 Diversity must be refocused to enable responsible organising

Janne Tienari and Jonna Louvrier

Introduction

This chapter argues that diversity must be refocused so that it does not blur responsibility in organisations and society. Diversity as a concept has allowed companies and other organisations to address questions of equality and inequality in ways that underscore both the business-related opportunities that a diverse workforce offers and the moral obligations that managing differences is grounded in. Diversity has offered a language that is accessible to practitioners and academics alike, and it has spurred many forms of meaningful collaboration. Diversity and inclusion have helped pave the way for gender equality (United Nations Sustainable Development Goal 5) and for reducing inequalities more generally (SDG 10).

However, as a concept and practice diversity has shortcomings and pitfalls. First, it does not address power relations and systemic dynamics of inequality unless it is carefully adapted to different socio-cultural and local contexts. Second, diversity is not only an artificial concept, but it serves to produce and reproduce a sense of lack among those who are cast as different and "diverse." It must be turned around to scrutinise those who exercise power in the name of diversity. Third, diversity is embedded in the historical and epistemic context of colonialism. It imposes Western epistemologies in categorising and representing the "diverse." The categories and labels used for construing the "diverse" need to be critically assessed in adaptations of diversity across the world.

We explore these potential pitfalls and map out ways to refocus diversity to tackle responsibility and social inequalities in the contemporary world. As such, we offer ideas on how a new understanding of diversity can enable responsible organising.

DOI: 10.4324/9781003229728-4

Diversity ignores power relations

As Jones, Pringle, and Shepherd (2000) and many others have argued, diversity does not address power relations in society. Diversity emerged as a concept in the USA in the 1980s to provide a means of managing what seemed like ever increasing dimensions of difference, from race and ethnicity to gender to age to sexual orientation and beyond (Johnston & Packer, 1987). Social inequalities identified by the civil rights, feminist, and gay rights movements in the preceding decades were addressed, but there was an apparent need to move from social divisions and justice to emphasising the positive aspects and manageability of difference. The notion of "diversity" was borrowed from biology to do this (Litvin, 1997). A domain of diversity knowledge developed to encompass ways and means to differentiate people (Nkomo & Hoobler, 2014) and diversity enabled decision-makers in organisations to render differences manageable through various tools and techniques of "diversity management" (Ahonen et al., 2014).

The idea of diversity and its management spread across the globe. Multinational corporations claimed diversity as a core value and public sector organisations and supranational entities such as the European Union embraced its rhetoric. In the process, a specific understanding of diversity was legitimised. US-based and other multinational corporations played a significant role in conceptualising diversity in an individualistic and meritocratic way (Holvino & Kamp, 2009). The assumption was that the Anglo-American notion of diversity (and its management) was readily applicable and adaptable irrespective of societal, cultural, or political conditions. However, diversity does not travel (Calás et al., 2009). It is difficult to root the diversity concept outside the Anglophone countries (Klarsfeld, 2010). The content and meanings given to diversity and its management need to be adapted to different sociocultural and local contexts.

Diversity and its management focus on, and emphasise, individuals and groups in organisations. The idea is based on the voluntary actions of organisational decision-makers to support diversity based on individuals and their assumed merits rather than, for example, affirmative action enforced by law. The concept of diversity runs the risk of transferring responsibility for treating human beings equally from democratic society to managerial decision-makers and shifting its rationale from social justice to instrumental business needs (Zanoni & Janssens, 2015). Diversity needs to address power relations and the systemic reproduction of inequalities and injustice in organisations and society.

Diversity represents "lack"

The idea of diversity as something through which individuals and groups can be consciously managed with universally applicable tools and techniques is a sign of globalisation through Anglo-American rhetoric. This is supposed to represent progress by supporting meritocracy and economic growth. A particular understanding of diversity is advocated, and for specific purposes: the business case argument is used to persuade managers to embrace a diverse workforce. It is emphasised that different skills, competences, and merits are attached to individuals with different diversity markers, and that the management of differences leads to enhanced performance through innovativeness and a better understanding of diverse customer needs (Thomas & Ely, 1996).

However, managing diversity with its scrutiny of ever multiplying markers of difference runs the risk of sustaining the status quo in organisations rather than challenging it. Ahonen and Tienari (2015) argue that the purpose of diversity practice and research is to identify objects that fit pre-set criteria. Whether the goal is organisational performance or social justice, what is required is identification, observation, and verification. Direct intervening action does not seem to be an integral part of the diversity apparatus, rather, it is first and foremost about monitoring differences. Diversity categories make it possible to identify, classify, and calculate, and to include and exclude (Ahonen & Tienari, 2015).

At the same time, diversity is an artificial concept. There is no absolute universal definition, just human beings with their appearances, characteristics, and idea(l)s (Omanović, 2010). Diversity can be used for window dressing and masking inequalities behind the façade of happy faces (Swan, 2010). However, diversity is not only artificial. The diverse are viewed in a frame of "lack" as they fail to meet organisational norms (Louvrier, 2013). In effect, diversity does not challenge the norm in organisations, but casts those who do not fit the norm as deviant, deficient, and diverse (Ostentorp & Steyaert, 2009). These people (are forced to) embody diversity (Ahmed, 2012).

Diversity becomes a mirror in which "diverse subjects" may find and align themselves with the categories forced upon them (Ahonen & Tienari, 2015). The diverse are supposed to embrace diversity and be empowered by the discursive resources provided. They are supposed to recognise their own lack and to act accordingly. Diversity runs the risk of blurring responsibility when it fails to address the norms it sustains in organisations. The gaze must be turned from those who are labelled "diverse" to those who exercise power in the name of diversity.

Diversity builds on colonialism

Diversity practice and research are arguably responses to the conditions that European colonialism of other parts of the world has produced (Greedharry et al., 2020). From the 15th century onwards, the expansion of European powers resulted not only in redistribution of global wealth, but also large-scale relocations of populations and decimation of peoples, environments, and cultures. It led to classifying and categorising people based on, for example, their "race" and "ethnicity." Colonialism changed the ways in which we think, make sense of, and relate to our world. Greedharry et al. (2020) argue that diversity continues to function within a colonial episteme, a way of thinking and producing knowledge about the world that is structured by colonial logic.

Taking colonialism seriously as the broad context for diversity is not only about acknowledging culturally different ways of knowing, but also about recognising and undoing the authority of the Global North to determine what diversity is and how we can know it (Greedharry et al., 2020). The enduring forms of colonial logic influence, organise, structure, and direct much of contemporary thinking on diversity. In many places around the globe, the populations from which organisations draw their workforce are the product, by-product, or an indirect consequence of colonialism. Much of diversity research addresses and aims to remedy the effects and injustices colonialism produced. At the same time, diversity research is a product of those colonial conditions. (Greedharry et al., 2020.) Diversity blurs responsibility in organisations and society when careful attention is not paid to the context and conditions in which diversity is drawn on to categorise and label people based on their "race," "ethnicity," and other characteristics.

Conclusion

The shortcomings and pitfalls of current understandings of diversity make a strong argument for refocusing it to better tackle questions of responsibility and social inequalities in the contemporary world. This means that we must:

- Address the systemic reproduction of inequalities and injustice in societies, and analyse how they play out in organisations.
- Examine power relations and the norms they sustain in societies and organisations, and scrutinise those who exercise power.

- Critically assess the categories and labels used for construing the "diverse" as well as the contextual conditions that enable such categorisation and labelling.

Diversity work in organisations can enable responsible organising if it is refocused. Those who do diversity work should:

- Define diversity based on a detailed analysis of the context where the organisation operates, and make sure that the definition does not ignore the structures that (re)produce power relations and inequalities there.
- Focus diversity work on those dimensions of difference that historically have made it difficult for members of certain groups to participate and contribute.
- Accept that there are no shortcuts to a long-term business case; diversity work is always courageous, and it challenges categories and labels and seeks to break existing discriminatory structures.

Through these changes on both the organisational and societal level, diversity can be refocused. Only by rethinking diversity in societally and locally sustainable ways can we organise responsibly for more social justice and equality across the world.

References

Ahmed, S. (2012) *On Being Included: Racism and Diversity in Institutional Life.* Durham, NC: Duke University Press.

Ahonen, P. & Tienari, J. (2015) Ethico-Politics of Diversity and Its Production. In *The Routledge Companion to Ethics, Politics and Organizations*, Eds. A. Pullen & C. Rhodes. London and New York, NY: Routledge, pp. 271–287.

Ahonen, P., Tienari, J., Meriläinen, S. & Pullen, A. (2014) Hidden contexts and invisible power relations: A Foucauldian reading of diversity research. *Human Relations* 67(3), 263–286. https://doi.org/10.1177/0018726713491772

Calás, M. B., Holgersson, C. & Smircich, L. (2009) Editorial: 'Diversity Management'? Translation? Travel? *Scandinavian Journal of Management* 25(4), 349–351. https://doi.org/10.1016/j.scaman.2009.09.006

Greedharry, M., Ahonen, P. & Tienari, J. (2020) Colonialism as Context in Diversity Research. In *The Routledge Companion to Organizational Diversity Research Methods*, Eds. S. Nørholm Just, A. Risberg & F. Villeseche. London: Routledge, pp. 13–23.

Holvino, E. & Kamp, A. (2009) Diversity management: Are we moving in the right direction? Reflections from both sides of the North Atlantic. *Scandinavian Journal of Management* 25(4), 395–403. https://doi.org/10.1016/j.scaman.2009.09.005

Johnston W. B. & Packer, A. E. (1987) *Workforce 2000. Work & Workers for the 21st Century*. Indianapolis, IN: Hudson Institute.

Jones D., Pringle J. & Shepherd, D. (2000) Managing diversity meets Aotearoa/ New Zealand. *Personnel Review* 29(3), 364–380. https://doi.org/10.1108/00483480010324715

Klarsfeld, A. (Ed) (2010) *International Handbook on Diversity Management at Work: Country Perspectives on Diversity and equal Treatment*. Cheltenham and Northampton, MA: Edward Elgar.

Litvin, D. R. (1997). The discourse of diversity: From biology to management. *Organization* 4(2), 187–209. https://doi.org/10.1177/135050849742003

Louvrier, J. (2013) *Diversity, Difference and Diversity Management: A Contextual and Interview Study of Managers and Ethnic Minority Employees in Finland and France*. Economics and Society – 259. Helsinki: Hanken School of Economics. http://hdl.handle.net/10138/40257.

Nkomo, S. M. & Hoobler, J. M. (2014) A historical perspective on diversity ideologies in the United States: Reflections on human resource management research and practice. *Human Resource Management Review* 24(3), 245–257. https://doi.org/10.1016/j.hrmr.2014.03.006

Omanović, V. (2011) Diversity in Organizations: A Critical Examination of the Assumptions about Diversity and Organizations in 21st Century Management Literature. In *The Handbook of Gender, Work and Organization*, Eds. E. Jeanes, D. Knights & P. Yancey Martin. London: Wiley.

Ostendorp, A. & Steyaert, C. (2009) How different can differences be(come)? Interpretive repertoires of diversity concepts in Swiss-based organizations. *Scandinavian Journal of Management* 25(4), 374–384. https://doi.org/10.1016/j.scaman.2009.09.003

Swan, E. (2010) Commodity diversity: Smiling faces as a strategy of containment. *Organization* 17(1), 77–100. https://doi.org/10.1177/1350508409350043

Thomas, D. A. & Ely, R. J. (1996) Making differences matter: A new paradigm for managing diversity. *Harvard Business Review* 74(5), 79–90.

Zanoni, P. & Janssens, M. (2015) The Power of diversity discourses at work: On the interlocking nature of diversities and occupations. *Organization Studies* 36(11), 1463–1483. https://doi.org/10.1177/0170840615593584

4 Responsibility is not only about humans

Maria Ehrnström-Fuentes and
Tiina Jääskeläinen

Introduction

This chapter develops the argument for viewing responsibility as a relational concept and construct based on humans' reciprocal relations to the nonhuman world and as an ability to respond and stay attuned to the world beyond ourselves. Responsible organising research increasingly acknowledges the role nonhumans (e.g., rivers, mountains, animals) play in acts of organising. The current planetary crises highlight previously ignored nonhuman others who through complex, enmeshed relations sustain the web of life on Earth (Ergene et al., 2021).

There has never been any organisation or organising process that does *not* include *any* nonhuman beings. They are part of organising in all situations. The reason that nonhumans are only now becoming visible in fields such as organisation and management studies is due to the disciplinary blinders of natural and social sciences, wherein nature is external and (human) organisations are seen as separate entities from the places and materialities that shape their existence. Research on organisations and organising is deeply influenced by ideas such as the Weberian rational/bureaucratic organisation (e.g., hierarchical structures, specialisation, predictability, and a rationality concept that separates humans and objects) and the Taylorist production management system (summarised by the "five M's": men, machines, methods, materials, and money). These ideas of what organisations and organising are about leave little room for theorising that includes nonhumans.

We use the word nonhuman in "a straight-forward, pragmatic sense that disrupts common, unconscious, anthropocentric associations with human to bring attention to the existence, agency, and necessity for respectful, relational consideration of beings who are not human" (Abbott, 2021, p. 1061). We make the distinction between nonhumans that participate in responsible organising in various ways

DOI: 10.4324/9781003229728-5

and "more-than-human organising" in which humans and nonhumans collectively partake in shaping responsibility. We discuss how different research traditions acknowledge the role of nonhumans in responsible organising and suggest engaging with Indigenous epistemes to move the discussion forward.

Nonhumans in research on responsible organising

Research traditions such as ecofeminism, ethics of care, and feminist new materialism (FNM) have made efforts to conceptualise the role of nonhumans in more-than-human responsible organising processes. This section gives a brief overview of how nonhumans have been addressed in these research traditions.

Ecofeminism

Ecofeminism is a philosophical grounding and an intellectual proposition that seeks to uncover the invisible structures and motivations that lead to domination over female/nonhuman bodies, while pointing at alternative forms of organising wherein human lives are connected to, and supportive of, the larger web of life (Mies & Shiva, 2014; Plumwood, 1993). Studies of responsible organising that draw on ecofeminism tend to focus on resistance to and consequences of environmentally destructive capitalist projects (Phillips, 2019) or envision alternative ways of organising that strive to address contemporary social and environmental challenges (Phillips & Jeanes, 2018). Nonhumans are not always the central piece of enquiry in these studies, rather they act as inspiration for authors writing about sustainability and ecology in relation to (responsible) organising.

Ethics of care

The ethics of care framework has its foundations in Carol Gilligan's book *In a Different Voice* (1982), which puts (human) relationships at the very heart of moral development. Tronto (1993) stresses the material dimension of how all humans and other life forms give or require care over their lifespans. Studies on responsible organising have used an ethics of care frame to show how affect, compassion, and other positive feelings are key to moral reflection, and have explored how such emotions influence both humans and nonhumans in their interwoven networks (Tallberg et al., 2021). Stressing the more-than-human material dimension, Beacham (2018) unpacks the entanglements of human and material elements within everyday practices of growing food by developing the notion of a more-than-human ethics of care (see also Puig de la Bellacasa, 2017). Such ethics of care make visible the human–earth relations that respect nature's temporality and its regeneration capacity (Beacham, 2018).

Feminist new materialism

FNM is influenced by feminist science and technology studies, posthumanist philosophy/ethics, environmental humanities, and affect studies (Braidotti, 2019). FNM acknowledges that humans are always (materially) enmeshed in more-than-human worlds (Barad, 2007; Haraway, 2016). Entities or bodies come into being through their relationship – in contrast to the usual notion of interaction that presumes the prior existence of independent entities and agencies (Barad, 2007). The term "response-ability" is used to emphasise the material, performative, and relational feature of how humans and nonhumans come into being and how they are rendered capable (of achieving agency to act) through situated and multidirectional relationships (Barad, 2007; Haraway, 2016). The aim of FNM is to disrupt the status quo of human exceptionalism and open spaces for re-imagining novel (or invisible) human–nonhuman entanglements that enable the making of different futures (Braidotti, 2019; Haraway, 2016).

Recent studies inspired by NFM show how nonhumans contribute to responsible organising. Davies and Riach (2019) show how the organising of beekeeping (and honey production) is constantly being "made" through multispecies practices of sustainability performed by humans, technologies, bees, and unwanted "pest" species. Influenced by Karen Barad's work, Gherardi and Laasch (2021) develop the notion of "responsible managing" as an ongoing accomplishment emerging from situated practices and mobilising particular knowledges of intra-actions that do (or do not) produce responsible effects on the world.

Indigenous epistemes

We argue for engaging with Indigenous epistemes to improve our understanding of human–nonhuman relations. Indigenous epistemes refer to the beliefs, assumptions, and ways of relating to the world that are shared by Indigenous peoples, acknowledging that human existence is embedded in a complex web of constantly evolving living relations (Kuokkanen, 2007). While most of the aforementioned research traditions (perhaps in some cases unknowingly) draw insights from Indigenous epistemes in conceptualising human–nonhuman relations, very few engage in depth with Indigenous more-than-human organising. Braidotti (2019) notes that much post-humanist research overlooks the knowledges of the "missing people," including the discriminatory/violent aspects of how some activities lead to the exclusion of others. This exclusion is an example of what Sámi scholar Rauna Kuokkanen calls epistemic ignorance. Kuokkanen (2007, p. 160) refers to epistemic ignorance as "the systems and mechanisms of exclusion, domination, and control in the academy all of which ensure that it remains impossible to hear indigenous epistemes." She maintains that "the academy adamantly opposes indigenous epistemes because they do not conform to its learned values about knowledge, rationality, and the world in general."

To dissolve epistemic ignorance, Kuokkanen (2007) suggests that academic scholars need to shift away from doing fieldwork "out there" towards learning from our own "homework"; asking ourselves how our own academic practices partake in the reproduction of epistemic ignorance. Doing our homework also involves fostering a deeper connection to the lands that sustain our own lives and recognising the gift of Indigenous epistemes to those lands in ways that transgress hegemonic knowledges and colonial superiority (Kuokkanen, 2007).

What is central to Indigenous epistemes is that the world is alive and active and that its various shapes and beings intelligently respond to and moderate human agency by making the world (more or less) liveable (Kuokkanen, 2007):

> Central to this perception is that the world as a whole is comprised of an infinite web of relationships that extend and are incorporated to the entire social condition of the individual. People are related to their physical and natural surroundings through their genealogies, their oral traditions and their personal and collective experiences with certain locations.
>
> (Kuokkanen, 2007, p. 32)

The wellbeing of humans, and sustaining their lives, depends on maintaining the right kind of relationships in balance with the cosmological whole that connects the material realm and all (human and non-human) living with other realms, including the spirit world and dead beings. The long-term well-being of mountains and rivers is inseparable from the well-being of people and their community (Kuokkanen, 2007). The relational features of Indigenous epistemes thus signify that response-ability towards the nonhumans is always grounded in place-based, reciprocal and circular relations of gift giving between humans and nonhumans. One does not give to receive (gifts as exchange), but to show gratitude and "ensure the balance of the world on which the well-being of the entire social order is contingent" (Kuokkanen, 2007, p. 33). Respect and gratitude are central notions of how Indigenous peoples relate to the more-than-human world. Thus, responsible organising in these contexts involves a complex entanglement of all interrelated life in a particular place, where the long-term well-being of the mountains, forests, and rivers is linked to the well-being of the community (Kuokkanen, 2007).

Indigenous epistemes ground responsible organising and the ability to respond to nonhumans in place. This profound (relational) approach to life does not embark on a speculative approach towards world-making (Barad, 2007; Haraway, 2016), but focuses on reciprocity and staying attuned to what the earth asks from us.

Conclusion

This chapter argues that responsible organising for a living earth depends on the intradependent reciprocal relations that people together with non-human actors hold towards each other while sustaining the wider web of life on our common planet. This needs to be recognised in all efforts to sustain the web of life on Earth. For example, how environmental sustainability has been constructed in the United Nations Sustainable Development Goals (particularly SDGs 13, 14, and 15) largely employs a human-centric lens that ignores more-than-human organising.

Research on responsible organising that includes nonhumans allows scholars to break free from the inherited blinders of our fields and immerse ourselves in inquiries that deal with living webs of relations. When we realise that our organisational success – staying alive and well on this planet – depends on how we connect with other creatures in the larger web of life, the questions we pose cease to centre on how to achieve efficiency and productivity at the expense of our web of life. Instead, novel questions appear. These include: Are our organisational efforts building life-affirming regenerative relations with the more-than-human world? In what way do our research methods and theories allow for circular reciprocity (through the logic of the gift) towards the living land that sustains us? How can research on responsible organising engage in reversing human-centred organising practices? What kind of inclusive more-than-human organisations have the capacity to restore the life-giving force of the web of life, while simultaneously overcoming inherited exclusionary structures?

We propose three steps forward through respectful engagement with Indigenous epistemes: (1) learning from the logic of the gift (based on reciprocity and gratitude), (2) homework rather than fieldwork to identify how academic practices reproduce colonial violence and epistemic ignorances, and (3) grounding research in place and responding to the living land that sustains our wellbeing and survival.

References

Abbott, S. (2021). Approaching nonhuman ontologies: Trees, communication, and qualitative inquiry. *Qualitative Inquiry*, *27*(8–9), 1059–1071. https://doi.org/10.1177/1077800421994954

Barad, K. (2007). *Meeting the universe halfway: Quantum physics and the entanglement of matter and meaning*. Duke University Press.

Beacham, J. (2018). Organising food differently: Towards a more-than-human ethics of care for the Anthropocene. *Organization*, *25*(4), 533–549. https://doi.org/10.1177/1350508418777893

Braidotti, R. (2019). *Posthuman knowledge*. Polity Press.

Davies, O., & Riach, K. (2019). From manstream measuring to multispecies sustainability? A gendered reading of bee-ing sustainable. *Gender, Work & Organization*, *26*, 246–266, https://doi.org/10.1111/gwao.12245

Ergene, S., Banerjee S. B., & Hoffman, A. J. (2021). (Un)Sustainability and organization studies: Towards a radical engagement. *Organization Studies*, *42*(8), 1319–1335. https://doi.org/10.1177/0170840620937892

Gherardi, S., & Laasch, O. (2021). Responsible management-as-practice: Mobilizing a posthumanist approach. *Journal of Business Ethics*. https://doi.org/10.1007/s10551-021-04945-7

Gilligan, C. (1982). *In a different voice: Psychological theory and women's development*. Harvard University Press.

Haraway, D. J. (2016). *Staying with the trouble: Making kin in the Chthulucene*. Duke University Press.

Kuokkanen, R. (2007). *Reshaping the university: Responsibility, Indigenous epistemes, and the logic of the gift*. UBC Press.

Mies, M., & Shiva, V. (2014). *Ecofeminism*. Zed Books.

Phillips, M. (2019). Daring to care": Challenging corporate environmentalism. *Journal of Business Ethics*, *156*, 1151–1164. https://doi.org/10.1007/s10551-017-3589-0

Phillips, M., & Jeanes, E. (2018). What are the alternatives? Organising for a socially and ecologically sustainable world. *Ephemera*, *18*(4), 695–708.

Plumwood, V. (1993). *Feminism and the mastery of nature*. Routledge.

Puig de la Bellacasa, M. (2017). *Matters of care – Speculative ethics in more than human worlds*. University of Minnesota Press.

Tallberg, L., García-Rosell, J. C., & Haanpää, M. (2021). Human–animal relations in business and society: Advancing the feminist interpretation of stakeholder theory. *Journal of Business Ethics*. https://doi.org/10.1007/s10551-021-04840-1

Tronto, J. C. (1993). *Moral boundaries: A political argument for an ethic of care*. Routledge.

Part II

Responsibility in a changing world

5   Global risks

Fundamentals are (not) changing

Wojciech D. Piotrowicz and Jana Abikova

Introduction

This chapter focuses on global risks and the supply chains critical for society, economy, and human lives. Responding to global risks is a necessary part of efforts to organise for sustainable outcomes, as expressed in the United Nations Sustainable Development Goals (SDGs). Already in 2006, pandemics were identified among the top risks by the World Economic Forum (WEF). Risks of climate change, extreme weather, natural disasters, and water crisis have prevailed alongside weapons of mass destruction, involuntary migration, failure of national governance, and unemployment (WEF, 2020). The risk of pandemics materialised in 2020 when the COVID-19 pandemic spread across the world. However, there is a variety of other risks that may sooner or later hit global society and economy that organisations need to consider in their preparedness and response plans.

Mega trends such as globalisation, population growth, migration, urbanisation, social inequality, and overconsumption have brought new challenges to the fore. As the globe is interconnected, many risks are systemic and global at the same time – they can change the system, or part of the system, as we know it. The interconnectivity of the world allows not only global growth but also global crises and failure, when disasters have cascading effects, spreading across the world. To analyse some of the current global risks we use the PMESII-PE framework (Walden, 2011), which includes risks assigned into seven dimensions: Political, Military, Economic, Social, Information, Infrastructure, and Physical Environment. The COVID-19 pandemic is discussed as an example of how the globalised world is, or is not, able to deal with the risks and challenges it is facing.

DOI: 10.4324/9781003229728-7

Risks in a globalised world

Risks are here reviewed in the order of the PMESII-PE framework: Political, Military, Economic, Social, Information, Infrastructure, and Physical Environment. However, it is important to note that risks are in practice interlinked and cover several dimensions at once.

Political

Fractures in interstate relations, resource geopolitics, competition, and state collapses are linked to political power struggles. These phenomena are not new, but still relevant, together with shifts in global power relations. One example is possible de-Europeanisation, tensions between the USA and China (see Chapter 6), as well as growing ambitions of regional players such as Turkey or Russia, leading to tensions with neighbouring countries and between political blocks. The rise and fall of countries are constant. They can be peaceful, as in the case of Czechoslovakia, or they can result in armed conflicts, as in Syria and Yemen.

Military

Conflicts between states, internal civil unrests, and tribal and religious conflicts leading to human rights violations and forced migration (Abikova & Piotrowicz, 2021) are as old as human history. A return of classic open conflict between states is not excluded as tensions may grow in Asia and Europe due to political change. What is new (or named as such) is a so-called unconventional or hybrid war conducted by states but also by different non-state actors, which use politics, disinformation, migration, and economic pressure to achieve political goals.

Economic

There is a shift in global economic power. New economies are growing rapidly while some others, formerly seen as having growth potential, struggle (SDG 8). Overconsumption (SDG 12) is problematic as it uses up resources (SDGs 14, 15) and deepens inequality (SDG 10). Although economic growth reduces poverty (SDG 1), it is linked with a negative impact on the environment, which causes economic loss and makes many global challenges worse in the longer term. At the same time, competition for resources is growing, including even water (SDG 6), and possibly food in the future (SDG 2), needed to sustain a growing population.

Social

Population growth is often mentioned as a social challenge. Although the world population continues to grow, changing levels of fertility and ageing of societies are happening at the same time, creating different challenges in different parts of the world, and stimulating migration. Another change in power arrangements is the emergence of various social movements and their power. Other social risks include the rise of individualism, the decline of social cohesion, and divisions within societies, caused by information bubbles (see Chapter 14).

Information

Information has become an asset that plays a crucial role in everything that happens in society. The rise of fake news that overlaps with misinformation and disinformation is becoming a global problem (Lazer et al., 2018) and a tool to achieve political, economic, and social goals. Information collection and sharing is a vital part of preparedness; misinformation may affect recovery processes in and between societies (WEF, 2021).

Infrastructure

Infrastructure is linked with population changes. On the one hand, due to population growth, there is demand for new infrastructure, and the existing one is under pressure (SDG 9). On the other hand, declining populations in some regions, like Europe, has the opposite effect and population ageing requires different types of services and infrastructure. At the same time global supply chains and information flows are highly dependent on transport and telecommunications infrastructure that may fail in face of man-made and natural disasters.

Physical environment

Climate change (SDG 13), extreme weather conditions, and natural disasters are among the risks related to the physical environment. Such changes may lead to food insecurity (SDG 2), leading to violent actions and conflicts in affected areas. Changes also boost migration, both national and international, and deepen inequality (SDG 10). They are also threatening infrastructure needed for business and society (SDG 9). Complex emergencies may appear when natural disasters and conflicts occur simultaneously.

Global risks and the COVID-19 pandemic

COVID-19 has had immense effects on health and well-being globally (SDG 3) but has also brought to the fore other risks related to global pandemics. The COVID-19 pandemic sped up trends like increased use of online communication, including for education and telemedicine. At the same time, in addition to the old risks, new ones are emerging, such as those related to technology, communication, and information systems dependency, but also a backlash against science and growth in inequality.

The COVID-19 pandemic threatens progress on reducing inequality (SDG 10) and global poverty (SDG 1). Inequality affects more than two-thirds of the global population. Four global forces affecting inequality are megatrends: climate change, urbanisation, international migration, and technological innovation. The fact that the poorest countries are disproportionately affected by disasters is partially the consequence of this inequality and lack of preparedness. Such countries are insufficiently equipped with early warning systems, they have few assets, weak social safety networks, and their infrastructure is not adequately resistant (Zorn, 2018). Also, poorer countries are more vulnerable to climate change (Nolan & Srinivasan, 2019). Inequality increases the risk of conflict and forces migration.

When responding to the COVID-19 pandemic, inequality has become apparent in vaccine distribution. According to the World Health Organisation (WHO), by January 2021 over 39 million vaccine doses had been given in 49 high-income countries, while only 25 doses had been administered in one low-income country (WHO, 2021b). WHO added that 75 per cent of early COVID-19 vaccines had been distributed in only ten countries, and almost 130 nations did not receive any vaccines at all (WHO, 2021a). The pandemic has also put pressure on healthcare systems, exposing their lack of capacity and inadequate preparedness. Hospitals were overwhelmed and countries had to deal with shortages of medical supplies (WEF, 2021).

The COVID-19 pandemic also has the potential to damage global cooperation and social cohesion. The pandemic has challenged both national policy-making and international relations (WEF, 2021). One example is the worsening US-China relationship that resulted when both states blamed each other for the spread of the virus and tried to shift global opinion in their favour (Gill, 2020).

The COVID-19 pandemic has been accompanied by a "massive infodemic" or growth in fake news and mass misinformation (Luengo & García-Marín, 2020). This points to the importance of information and fact-checking. Social media platforms like Facebook, Twitter, Google, and YouTube have been full of misleading information, conspiracy theories, and fake news surrounding the global pandemic, discrediting scientific research. However, COVID-19 has also revealed that many people search for reliable and trustworthy information, bringing more opportunities for professional journalism (Luengo & García-Marín, 2020) and science.

The COVID-19 pandemic has demonstrated the way the world is – a globalised world on one planet. For years, experts and activists have been trying to show that climate change is a risk for life on the planet. The same is true for the COVID-19 pandemic. These two global challenges for humanity have much in common: it is necessary to act before it is too late, science and facts matter, innovation is key, international collaboration is needed, and they remind us that we coexist with nature (Jin, 2020).

While addressing climate change has been slow, COVID-19 affected the daily life of all citizens and appeared more "real," thus boosting research, cooperation between states, cities, and individuals, and solidarity after initial competition and focus on national interests. For example, vaccines against COVID-19 were developed after very short research and testing, then produced and distributed through global supply chains, though initially to developed countries. There have been cases of cross-border medical support for countries with weaker medical systems, and humanitarian organisations have changed their operations towards COVID-19 responsiveness.

Overall, while the pandemic has exposed weaknesses, it has also brought new opportunities for global change to the fore. One example is digitalisation, as it became a way to adapt to a "new normal" in 2020–2021. Digitalisation enabled to develop online education. The pandemic also helped to design new prevention measures, like drive-through testing, and products, such as testing kits. Companies got a chance to contribute by adopting corporate social responsibility initiatives and enhancing their reputation. Some manufacturers also restructured their global supply chains making them more sustainable (Liu et al., 2020).

Conclusion

Risks are changing, while fundamentally staying the same. Global risks are similar as decades and centuries ago. These include politics, conflict, competition, and fight for power. What is new is the emergence of the global system where countries and regions are interconnected by political, trade, and supply chain networks. This interconnectedness, and often interdependence, represents a new challenge due to the fragility it causes to the globalised world, when crisis in one part of the world has cascading effects and spreads across the globe, as in the case of the COVID-19 pandemic. The current global system is not prepared well to respond to such systemic risks.

Understanding and acknowledging global risks is the first step for responsibly organising for sustainable outcomes. While it is impossible to eliminate all risks, it is possible to mitigate them, through cooperation in initiatives such as the SDGs. Competition between countries is inevitable, but open conflict is possible to avoid. Responsible organising at the political, economic, and social levels can prevent the materialisation of many global risks. Accepting both personal and organisational accountability and one's own role and power to initiate change is always the first step.

Acknowledgements

This work was supported by the Academy of Finland (grant number: 322188).

References

Abikova, J., & Piotrowicz, W. (2021). Shaping the Balkan corridor: Development and changes in the migration route 2015–16. *International Migration, 59*, 248–265. https://doi.org/10.1111/imig.12828

Gill, B. (2020). China's global influence: Post-COVID prospects for soft power. *The Washington Quarterly*, 43(2), 97–115. https://doi.org/10.1080/0163660X.2020.1771041

Jin, S. (2020). COVID-19, climate change, and renewable energy research: we are all in this together, and the time to act is now. *ACS Energy Letters*, 5(5), 1709–1711. https://doi.org/10.1021/acsenergylett.0c00910

Lazer, D. M., Baum, M. A., Benkler, Y., Berinsky, A. J., Greenhill, K. M., Menczer, F., ... & Zittrain, J. L. (2018). The science of fake news. *Science*, 359(6380), 1094–1096. https://doi.org/10.1126/science.aao2998

Liu, Y., Lee, J. M., & Lee, C. (2020). The challenges and opportunities of a global health crisis: the management and business implications of COVID-19 from an Asian perspective. *Asian Business & Management*, 1. https://doi.org/10.1057/s41291-020-00119-x

Luengo, M., & García-Marín, D. (2020). The performance of truth: politicians, fact-checking journalism, and the struggle to tackle COVID-19 misinformation. *American Journal of Cultural Sociology*, 8(3), 405–427. https.//doi.org/10.1057/s41290-020-00115-w

Nolan, S. & Srinivasan, K. (2019). *Poorer countries are more vulnerable to climate change – here's how they can prepare.* Retrieved from World Economic Forum website: www.weforum.org/agenda/2019/07/when-disaster-strikes-preparing-for-climate-change

Walden, J. (2011*).* *Comparison of the STEEPLE Strategy Methodology and the Department of Defense's PMESII-PT Methodology.* Retrieved from Supply Chain Research Institute website: http://supplychainresearch.com/images/Walden_Strategy_Paper.pdf (Date of request: 07.10. 2020).

World Economic Forum. (2006). *The Global Risks Report 2006.* Retrieved from World Economic Forum website: www3.weforum.org/docs/WEF_Global_Risks_Report_2006.pdf

World Economic Forum. (2020). *The Global Risks Report 2020.* Retrieved from World Economic Forum website: www.weforum.org/reports/the-global-risks-report-2020

World Economic Forum. (2021). *The Global Risks Report 2021.* Retrieved from World Economic Forum website: www3.weforum.org/docs/WEF_The_Global_Risks_Report_2021.pdf

World Health Organization. (2021a). *WHO Director-General's opening remarks at the 148th session of the Executive Board.* Retrieved from World Health Organization website: www.who.int/director-general/speeches/detail/director-general-s-opening-remarks-at-the-world-health-assembly---24-may-2021

World Health Organization. (2021b). *Director-General's opening remarks at the World Health Assembly – 24 May 2021.* Retrieved from World Health Organization website: www.who.int/director-general/speeches/detail/who-director-general-s-opening-remarks-at-148th-session-of-the-executive-board

Zorn, M. (2018). Natural disasters and less developed countries. In Pelc, S. & Koderman, M. (eds), *Nature, tourism and ethnicity as drivers of (De) marginalization. Perspectives on Geographical Marginality*, vol 3. (pp. 59–78). Springer, Cham. https://doi.org/10.1007/978-3-319-59002-8_4.

6 Re-emergence of geopolitics and façades of responsibility

Mikko Vesa, Ling Eleanor Zhang, and Ya Xi Shen

Introduction

This chapter highlights the return of global geopolitics. In his famous book "The End of History and the Last Man" Francis Fukuyama (1991) predicted that with the fall of the Soviet Union the world had moved to a stage where systemic competition between global power blocs had come to an end. The Western, liberal-democratic market economy model had survived to be the last man standing. It would be just a matter of time before the whole globe would come to heel before the only viable remaining systemic alternative. Fukuyama predicted a similar end to the major dimension of geopolitics, "the struggle over the control of geographical entities with an international and global dimension, and the use of such geographical entities for political advantage" (see Flint, 2017, p. 16 for a full definition). With the unfair advantage of hindsight, Fukuyama's observation is turning out to be somewhat premature, although in all fairness he has defended the stance that the notion of the end of history was originally positioned as a question (Fukuyama, 2018). Whilst the Cold War indeed did end in 1991, history itself, it turns out, had no aptitude for endings.

What we have witnessed is an interregnum of some 20 to 30 years when the system to which Fukuyama attributed victory ruled supreme on the global arena. The Global North (or West) controlled both the global institutional framework, business and finance, as well as critical areas of scientific and cultural production. This interregnum could be characterised as a state of hegemony where system-threatening critique of the prevailing system was marginalised into small circles of activists and intellectuals. However, somewhere in the process, wider resistance crept into the picture. Hegemony often comes with this quality of instability in the face of time. Sociologists Krastev and Holmes (2019) attribute this to a growing sense of frustration amongst both the

DOI: 10.4324/9781003229728-8

leadership but also the citizens of many former second and third world countries: a frustration born out of a sense of always being at best second to the Global North that one was trying to emulate and catch up with. We argue that the economic ascendancy of China is turning into a major pivoting point in this regard. This is important for studies on responsible organising because it calls into question both what it means to be responsible and towards whom one should be responsible. Responsibility will increasingly be played out with at least two different sets of cards.

China and resistance to Western hegemony

While the Global North was celebrating the end of the Cold War, in the People's Republic of China, the economy was positively thundering ahead by exploiting new-found access to global markets and foreign direct investment. The interregnum was the era of the globalisation imperative when states were prepared to endure almost anything to cajole at the fine dinner table of the Global North. Meanwhile, it appeared that the Global North, especially in Europe, was rapidly deconstructing the bases of its own internal success, namely the welfare state and an inclusive society for all citizens. What, however, for long went unnoticed by the global party's Western hosts was that the adherence to the evening's dress code was increasingly superficial and in the case of China probably never existed in the first place.

The resistance to Western hegemony initially manifested itself as increasing nationalism. The political landscape of countries such as Russia and India, but also widely across Eastern Europe, changed. To some extent, the triumph of Donald Trump in the 2016 presidential election signalled USA's loss of faith in the very system they championed. However, to accrue a quality contesting Fukuyama's verdict requires a systemic challenge. It is here that China becomes critically important.

Until the ascendancy of Xi Jinping and 5th generation leadership in 2013, China had for decades followed a policy established in the late 1970s by then-paramount leader Deng Xiaoping emphasising the keeping of a low profile and pursuing economic modernisation. In 2013, this stance changed. Xi declared the Chinese system as superior, and its survival a life-and-death question for the Chinese nation (Economy, 2018, p. 6). This begs the question of "superior to whom?" and if the West as the obvious target of Xi's critique recognised the challenge. The EU declared China a systemic rival in 2019, whilst newly elected US President Joseph Biden maintained the more assertive China policy established by his predecessors, characterising the USA–China relation as one of extreme competition. History was back, geopolitics had returned, and suddenly also multinational corporations were whisked into the trenches of souring global relations.

Geopolitics as technology regimes

There is high-profile evidence of souring relations that are the result of re-emerging geopolitics. Perhaps the most prominent example is the struggle around the Chinese mobile communications giant Huawei, whose products and services have been labelled as security risks in an increasing number of Western countries. Many technology companies from China face similar constraints. At the same time, Beijing is beginning to curtail efforts by mainland technology companies to list themselves on Western stock exchanges, typically quoting concerns with how these companies treat data confidentiality. Whilst potentially over-dramatising the current situation, it is tempting to draw comparisons to the Cold War era when NATO strictly regulated technology exports to the "Eastern bloc" countries, severely curtailing the Soviet Union's access to new key technologies such as microchips.

It is worthwhile to ask if the new geopolitics will result in a similar fragmentation of technology development globally into one camp centred around USA and another centred around China? However, in contrast to the Cold War, the main driver for the emergence of this new technological divide can be found in business logics. Namely, the risk of crossing the political barrier with its ensuing sanctions can be so high that companies operating in the extremely competitive landscape of today simply are not willing to take the risks involved. This is the economic face of geopolitics: corporate self-imposed de-globalisation (and consequently, re-regionalisation) of our economic and technological interconnectedness.

The interesting question that we are facing with a possibly re-emerging technological divide is, how deep will it go? Will techno-nationalism (Petricevic & Teece, 2019) remain a matter of governmental give-and-take in which control over technology is handled pragmatically to discipline companies, or will we begin to see the formation of separate technology regimes in which national or regional clusters of hardware and software developers bundle up their efforts to create regional, and over time potentially very different, technological infrastructures? Will such infrastructures accrue distinct political and cultural characteristics in fields such as artificial intelligence, resulting in distinct understandings of what technology can accomplish and how it is morally permissible to wield technology?

We are seeing in the Global North a strong response, even outcry, to how China is using advanced technology for monitoring and control of society. In China, the same technology is seen as important for re-establishing trust within and amongst citizens. Ultimately, this comes down to what rules and roles are allotted to data – the fuel of the digital economy and society – in different technological regimes.

What might appear at first as a de-globalisation challenge confronting international business actors such as multinational corporations and global regulators, comes down to more fundamental questions of culture, norms, and the ethics of society. The façades of responsibility that this entails is largely a question of a legitimacy struggle between the major actors of our times over which ideal society to pursue, a legitimacy struggle now largely split between the Global North and China. Façades of responsibility implies the geopolitical struggle to both control the agenda setting on responsibility and to appear as the leading responsible actor. As China's challenge to the Global North strengthens, it will desire to promote its own standards in this. Regardless of the specific actors, controlling responsibility is a source of legitimacy and power but we should understand that the desire to control legitimacy can have rather utilitarian motives rather than truly aspire to sustainability. Hence, what we see as responsibility is often just the façade of the power game.

Yet, the paradoxical legacy of 30 years of Western hegemony is that whilst the world is trying to disentangle its interdependencies, it is still a world that is interconnected in many and complex ways. Several of the sustainability challenges that we face do not have agreed-upon solutions that can be enacted on local or regional levels. Rather, they will need to be addressed through common frameworks, platforms, and institutions on which potentially conflicting interpretations of ideal social values are capable of co-existing, interacting, and even achieving consensus.

Conclusion

Based on our analysis of global geopolitics, we propose that the United Nations Sustainable Development Goals (SDGs) can play a mediating role in easing the geopolitical conflicts that appear to be emerging, for example, between USA and China. Their meanings and the operationalisation of action that they generate will be subject to constant struggles involving the façades of responsibility regarding the desirability of specific interpretations. At the same time, they offer a table for dialogue on issues which need to be solved for the common good of the planet. The SDGs themselves can be understood as topics for negotiation, which through their collective acknowledgement by parties inherently at odds form the possibility for not only "strengthening the means of implementation and revitalise the global partnership for sustainable development" (SDG 17) but for creating dialogue for sufficient common understanding of what sustainability must entail.

Whilst the role of the United Nations, contested by both unilateralism and regionalism, has appeared to be diminishing since the end of the Cold War, it is an interesting observation to remember that the UN in many ways was an institution for that era. Perhaps the UN will find itself relevant once more exactly when the world is heading for a new era of divisions? Just like in earlier times, major state actors require common institutions through which to signal their differences even when attempting to find common ground.

References

Economy, E. (2018). *The third revolution: Xi Jinping and the new Chinese state.* Oxford: Oxford University Press.

Flint, C. (2017). *Introduction to geopolitics*, 3rd edition. London: Routledge.

Fukuyama, F. (1991). *The end of history and the last man.* New York, NY: Simon and Schuster.

Fukuyama, F. (2018). *Identity: Contemporary identity politics and the struggle for recognition.* London: Profile Books.

Krastev, I., & Holmes, S. (2019). *The light that failed: A reckoning.* London: Penguin.

Petricevic, O., & Teece, D. J. (2019). The structural reshaping of globalization: Implications for strategic sectors, profiting from innovation, and the multinational enterprise. *Journal of International Business Studies*, 50(9), 1487–1512. https://doi.org/10.1057/s41267-019-00269-x

7   Cross-sector collaborations for responsibility

Visa Penttilä and Frank den Hond

Introduction

This chapter argues that responsible organising is not limited to managing intra-organisational matters to bring about beneficial outcomes regarding social and environmental aspirations. We turn our attention to cross-sector collaborations for corporate social responsibility and discuss how such actions can be organised in novel ways. The United Nations Sustainable Development Goals (SDGs) provide admirable targets for governments, businesses, and civil society. However, they also paint a simplified picture of the means to achieve these goals: they rely on voluntary measures, such as global partnerships, to address complex problems. Moreover, even when voluntary measures can provide impetus towards sustainable development, the organising of such endeavours may be difficult. Actors with incompatible interests might have a hard time finding common ground for their efforts.

The responsibility of companies is a case in point as they may lack interest in taking voluntary actions for sustainable development. In this chapter, we argue that the SDGs can be pushed further with collective political action that aims at regulating corporate conduct. To explore how organising such action can take place, we present the empirical case of a cross-sector coalition that aimed at initiating such a regulatory process in Finland. This case elucidates responsible organising as a relational activity that aligns interests of different organisations for sustainable development.

The potential of cross-sector coalitions

SDG 17 aims to "strengthen the means of implementation and revitalise the global partnership for sustainable development." It can be considered a steppingstone towards more permanent solutions for

DOI: 10.4324/9781003229728-9

sustainable development when such partnerships provide impetus for regulatory initiatives. While there are various voluntary collaborative actions aimed at solving social and environmental problems, such collaborations are but one organisational vehicle for achieving sustainable outcomes. Organisational coalitions stand out as key alternatives for advancing more permanent solutions (Brooker & Meyer, 2018), especially when they aim at promoting regulation of social and environmental issues.

In general, initiatives for regulating corporate responsibilities are important for achieving SDGs, as the negative impacts of corporate activities need to be addressed. The United Nations Guiding Principles for Business and Human Rights (UNGPs) provide a complementary framework for considering how these negative impacts can be alleviated, for example, by conducting human rights due diligence (HRDD) in supply chains (Buhmann et al., 2019). HRDD refers to the continuous processes of evaluating an organisation's human rights impacts, taking measures to address any issues, and communicating on these matters (United Nations, 2011). Part of the UNGPs is the use of corporate leverage for alleviating human right violations, which can be considered as potential means for achieving SDGs.

However, getting companies to support regulatory measures can be difficult. Businesses are often seen either as being opposed to regulation or as apolitical entities that are not involved in policy making. However, this is hardly the whole truth: corporate lobbying may also be supportive of new or stricter regulation. Companies that are already implementing practices to take care of their social and environmental impacts can derive competitive advantages from stricter regulation, aligning their corporate responsibility and political action strategies (den Hond et al., 2014). Moreover, companies that consider themselves as apolitical often engage in politics at arms-length as members of industry associations that lobby on behalf of their members.

Nevertheless, the number of instances in which companies are first in line to promote regulation for sustainable development remains relatively modest. Civil society actors are far more active in such matters, as they can provide both pressure and expertise for decision-makers (Beyers et al., 2009). Harnessing corporate political action through cross-sector collaborations between civil society actors and companies can be beneficial for both. For companies, coalitions can offer a convenient way to promote particular policies. They can have an impact with only limited investments, and by being a part of a wider group of organisations retain a distance from the actual lobbying and thereby reduce the risk of a public opinion backlash. For non-governmental organisations (NGOs), collaborating with companies can provide both resources and legitimacy in the eyes of politicians who might find a demand for regulation more convincing when it is endorsed by a more diverse set of actors.

Of course, cross-sector coalitions or partnerships do not appear "just like that"; they need to be carefully organised (Bryson et al., 2006). In particular, the goal setting of such constellations merits consideration, as cross-sector collaborations involve divergent interests. In addition, understanding the strategies of such coalitions is essential. The 2×2 framework by Colli and Adriaensen (2020) can be used for classifying these strategies. Their framework distinguishes activities that target markets from those that target the state. Regarding both targets, coalitions can use "inside" and "outside" strategies. Inside strategies target markets or the state through personal relations and cooperation, whereas outside strategies build public pressure towards them with the help of voters and consumers. Understanding how such strategies work in practice can provide insights into organising for sustainable outcomes in the context of regulatory initiatives.

Cross-sector coalition "#To the first line"

To empirically explore the arguments above, we offer the example of *#ykkösketjuun (#to the first line)*, a Finnish cross-sector coalition coordinated by Finnish watchdog NGO Finnwatch that successfully campaigned for initiating a review on the possibility of HRDD legislation in Finland under the 2019 parliamentary elections. While the substance of HRDD is based on the UNGPs and addresses sustainable development in a different way from the SDGs, the coalition that we examine shows how effective partnerships can be built in the spirit of SDG 17. To provide useful insights into responsible organising, we focus on two aspects of this voluntary, cross-sector collaboration: its goal setting and its strategies of political action. In terms of the Colli and Adriaensen (2020) framework, the coalition was able to enlist companies, labour unions, and various civil society organisations to jointly target the state. It used "inside" strategies in recruiting companies to the coalition and then in lobbying candidates for all major political parties, and "outside" strategies in mustering support from the general public.

Goal setting

When building a multi-organisational coalition, the goal of the coalition is a major consideration. However, given the ambitious nature of

SDGs it is important to analyse how a particular goal can be set and made to work in a context where highly divergent interests are present.

The #ykkösketjuun coalition aimed at initiating a legislative process for regulating how companies are to take care of the human rights impacts of their own activities, as well as those of their suppliers. Rather than relying on corporate actors to take voluntary measures on these matters, it aimed at regulating corporate action through legislation. The goal setting revolved around balancing an ambitious and concrete enough target with a broad enough coalition composition to gain popular appeal. These dimensions can be seen as inversely related: the more specific and ambitious the goal, the less support for the goal can be expected, as individual organisations may not share similar views on the specifics and they may be averse to support a target deemed unachievable.

Given these conditions, the initial coalition composed of NGOs decided to lobby for a statement regarding HRDD regulation in the governmental programme. Finland has a multi-party political system and a tradition of coalition governments. The governmental programme is negotiated among the parties that form the government after the parliamentary elections, detailing its legislative agenda. A statement in this document means an important step towards legislation. However, the coalition refrained from defining specifically what should be the exact content of the legislation, nor did it push for taking it beyond the statement in the governmental programme. The goal was to push HRDD one critical step forward as a unified coalition. By limiting the goal of the coalition, it enabled individual participants to pursue their own specific goals after the campaign ended. For example, if an NGO had specific suggestions for the legislation, they could provide those suggestions for the government later if, and when, the actual legislative process started.

The goal setting enabled the coalition to recruit not only wide support from NGOs and labour unions, but also from companies (70 in total), including the two largest retailers in the country. For many of these companies it was of utmost importance that the coalition would not promote a specific content for the regulation as a coalition, as both NGOs and companies deemed the specifics too divisive. This shows how even a relatively small-scale cross-sector coalition necessitated limited goal setting. In the context of SDGs this finding can be interpreted as a reminder of the inherent complexity involved in cross-sector collaborations. The interests of different actors need to be carefully accommodated if they are to rally behind a common cause for sustainable development, such as the ones specified in the SDGs.

Strategies of political action

To achieve its chosen goal, the #ykkösketjuun coalition employed a variety of strategies for political action. While strength in numbers provided credibility for the action (altogether 144 organisations), this also enabled efficient "inside" lobbying. With a large number of organisations there were more human resources and more contacts at individual and organisational levels. The diverse composition of the coalition ensured that the lobbying could be tailored to different parties. For example, certain NGOs were closer with some political parties, enabling natural points of contact, while corporate representatives could meet with politicians who entertain market-oriented values.

The lobbying was also inclusive in terms of who was lobbied. As Finland has a multi-party system, there was no way of knowing which parties would form the new coalition government. In order to manage this uncertainty, the coalition decided to promote HRDD to all the major parties, striving to keep the matter as non-partisan as possible. This ensured that any particular party could not hijack the cause for themselves.

The political action was not, however, limited to "inside" strategies. For example, the coalition ran a public campaign collecting over 10,000 signatures in support of HRDD regulation. While this "outside" strategy increased the visibility of the campaign among citizens and politicians, the aforementioned inside lobbying was more important for the coalition's success as it ensured the commitment of the parliamentary candidates to HRDD. The coalition's efforts resulted in the newly negotiated government including a HRDD act in its programme, making the coalition successful in reaching its goal.

These strategies provide insights how to push the SDGs further. As SDGs are adopted by all UN member states, and many companies are publicly committed to them, they could potentially provide non-partisan steppingstones towards regulatory solutions. Moreover, it is feasible to direct cross-sector efforts towards inside lobbying strategies for SDG-related issues rather than just voicing public support for the goals themselves in order to push for more permanent solutions.

Conclusion

Our chapter has shown that responsible organising for the SDGs can be done with aims that go over and above the partnerships that are participating in such actions. Pushing for regulation to affect how companies conduct themselves has potential effects beyond any single collaboration. We suggest that organisations that operate in the framework of the SDGs consider how to push the goals further with political action. While this may seem somewhat of a challenging proposition, we want to emphasise that political action for corporate responsibility in the spirit of SDG 17 need not be black and white – it can take forms of joining petitions and giving support to organisations that actively promote these matters in other ways.

Acknowledgements

This research has received funding from the Academy of Finland (grant number: 325768).

References

Beyers, J., Eising, R., & Maloney, W. (2009). Researching interest group politics in Europe and elsewhere: Much we study, little we know? *West European Politics*, 31(6), 1103–1128. https://doi.org/10.1080/01402380802370443.

Brooker, M. E., & Meyer, D. (2018). Coalitions and the organization of collective action. In: Snow, D. A., Soule, S. A., Kriesi, H., & McCammon, H. J. (Eds.), *The Wiley Blackwell Companion to Social Movements* (2nd Ed.), pp. 252–268. London: John Wiley & Sons. https://doi.org/10.1002/9781119168577.ch14.

Bryson, J. M., Crosby, B. C., & Stone, M. M. (2006). The design and implementation of cross-sector collaborations: Propositions from the literature. *Public Administration Review*, 66, 44–55. https://doi.org/10.1111/j.1540-6210.2006.00665.x.

Buhmann, K., Jonsson, J., & Fisker, M. (2019). Do no harm and do more good too: Connecting the SDGs with business and human rights and political CSR theory. *Corporate Governance*, 19(3), 389–403. https://doi.org/10.1108/CG-01-2018-0030.

Colli, F., & Adriaensen, J. (2020). Lobbying the state or the market? A framework to study civil society organizations' strategic behavior. *Regulation & Governance*, 14(3), 501–513. https://doi.org/10.1111/rego.12227.

den Hond, F., Rehbein, K. A., de Bakker, F. G. A., & Kooijmans-van Lankveld, H. (2014). Playing on two chessboards: Reputation effects between corporate social responsibility (CSR) and corporate political activity (CPA). *Journal of Management Studies*, 51(5), 790–813. https://doi.org/10.1111/joms.12063.

United Nations (2011). *Guiding Principles on Business and Human Rights. Implementing the United Nations "Protect, Respect and Remedy" Framework*. New York, NY: United Nations Office of the High Commissioner for Human Rights. Available from: www.unglobalcompact.org/library/2.

8 The ecosystem approach to responsibility

*Kaisa Penttilä, Man Yang, and
Ashkan Fredström*

Introduction

This chapter discusses the ecosystem approach to responsibility in tackling climate change (United Nations Sustainable Development Goal, SDG 13) and other sustainability challenges. After centuries of industrialisation, we can no longer ignore the impact that human beings and our actions have on the environment. We must act now to synchronise with the nature around us. This is reflected in recent political movements such as the Paris agreement and the EU's goal of becoming climate neutral by 2050.

One important area in becoming climate neutral is to make energy production, distribution, and consumption more environmentally friendly (SDG 7). The EU and other regions in the world have invested heavily in the development of renewable energy sources (e.g., wind and solar), and their production has become viable without governmental subsidies. However, challenges are still to be addressed. To overcome the challenges there is a need for invested efforts of a multitude of actors. Single individuals, companies, or even nations do not possess the resources to organise the system level solutions that can tackle the sustainability challenges. Rather, partnerships between actors (SDG 17) are required.

A critical question for organising the system level solutions for sustainability is how to orchestrate multiple actors in order to realise the sustainable value propositions. We introduce the ecosystem approach to organising system level solutions that tackle sustainability challenges. This approach takes a structural view and looks at how the combination of complementary resources and activities from different actors can create ecosystem-wide value propositions (Adner, 2017; Hannah & Eisenhardt, 2018). We define ecosystems as "the alignment structure of the multilateral set of partners that need to interact in order for a focal

DOI: 10.4324/9781003229728-10

value proposition to materialize" (Adner, 2017, p. 40). We propose the ecosystem approach to responsibility for both business and non-business actors to consider how their activities can be combined to organise for sustainability. We present the case of green hydrogen as an example of how the ecosystem approach can be implemented in practice.

Conventional versus the ecosystem approach to responsibility

Conventional approaches to responsibility applied by companies have strong roots in strategic management, which involves the formulation and implementation of the major sustainability goals and initiatives taken by an organisation (e.g., Corporate Social Responsibility, or CSR). These often focus on what a focal actor's strategy is towards outside actors and how it enhances its own legitimacy or competitive capabilities. CSR can be problematic due to the business and focal actor centric approach to responsibility and sustainability. It concerns how the company as an economic actor can benefit (e.g., in terms of brand or image) from socially and environmentally responsible activities and in this way *also* do good for the society. As indicated in Chapter 2, the main positive impact of CSR is often on business, not on society. This can be remedied if CSR is applied through business-aligned stakeholder actions, such as cross-sector partnerships. However, what makes such partnerships long-lasting and fruitful for sustainability is not answered by conventional approaches.

An ecosystem approach (Aarikka-Stenroos & Ritala, 2017) offers a new perspective on responsibility. At the heart of this approach lies the focus on realising value propositions that could not materialise without a set of partners having a joint value creation effort as their mutual goal. An ecosystem approach centred on value propositions deals with "the promised benefit that the target of the effort is to receive," and the activities and actors involved in bringing this about (Adner, 2017, p. 43). It provides a lens to analyse who the value creating actors are, what the structure of multilateral interactions is, and how different actors must be aligned so that a focal value proposition will materialise (Adner, 2017). The ecosystem approach pays attention to how actors' activities are organised around sustainable value propositions, which may result in system level sustainable solutions and outcomes.

Ecosystem orchestration is a key task that needs a dedicated actor with the required capabilities for the task and a socio-technical environment that is malleable enough for the ecosystem value proposition in question (Walrave et al., 2018). As Jonker et al. (2020, p. 20) noted, "[i]f parties in a particular region can collaborate from the beginning with sufficient scale, and if this collaboration has an ideal-typical integral character, then the scale of transition and collective value creation will coincide." This requires a high amount of trust and "win-win-win" thinking among the actors that are about to collaborate. Win-win-win implies that all involved partners gain benefit from contributing to the ecosystem value proposition. Ecosystems as such are not bounded by physical location, since they can also operate in a fully digital environment, such as mobile application platforms (Jacobides et al., 2018). However, there is indication from research that projects at the regional level are most likely to succeed for industrial "niche development" paths, such as the green hydrogen solution discussed in this chapter, because both physical and cultural proximity enhance the willingness to engage in building value propositions on the ecosystem level (Penttilä et al., 2020).

Towards the ecosystem approach: the case of green hydrogen

Companies often approach creating a sustainable value proposition by investing in making their products or services carbon dioxide (CO_2) neutral. In such cases, value creating activities are arranged through transactional interactions with other actors and hierarchical relationships between a deliverer and a receiver of value. However, the sustainability challenges of today's world cannot be tackled with single efforts of individual companies. For example, a company can offer a car that produces zero emissions, but if the infrastructure is not in place for maintaining and servicing that car, if there is no appropriate fuel or no chance of refuelling it at convenient locations, or if there are no tax benefits for changing to it from a more polluting vehicle, the value proposition does not materialise for a citizen owning the car or for the city having a CO_2 neutrality target. Thus, an ecosystem approach is needed to make system level changes when multiple actors are aligned in ways where every actor has a complementary role and position, and their interactions are orchestrated in ways that contribute to the sought-after system level changes.

The energy transition, moving away from fossil-based fuels and replacing them with renewables, is a timely case of the type of system level challenges that call for an ecosystem approach to responsibility (European Commission, 2020). At the system level, wind and solar energy are seen as the key enablers of transitioning into fossil free energy production systems in the future. Due to the weather-dependent character of producing wind and solar energy, there is a need to find efficient solutions for short- and long-term energy storage as well as for the conversion of the stored energy back to usable forms.

One of the solutions, which is gaining increasing momentum, is green hydrogen (H_2). Hydrogen has characteristics that promise to make it widely produced and used for different applications. Electricity produced by, for example, wind and solar energy can be converted into hydrogen. The hydrogen can then be used, for example, in fuel cells used in transportation, as a substitute for coke in the steel industry, or as an essential reactant at the basis of many chemical products (Nižetić et al., 2021; Rambhujun et al., 2020). Green hydrogen is a substance that is both produced from water and dissolves into water as it is burnt, which makes it a superior substance in terms of its non-polluting characteristic.

Actors from the Ostrobothnia region in Finland announced in January 2021 that they will start cooperating on the world's first green hydrogen production, storage, and energy reconversion system. The partners, consisting of (1) a global technology company in marine and energy, (2) a national energy company, (3) a utility company supplying electricity and district heating, and (4) the local city, are to jointly build and demonstrate an innovative "Power-to-X-to-Power" system (see Figure 8.1). At the core of the collaboration is commitment from all partners to advance the decarbonisation of their respective sectors. The goals and activities of each actor can be described in basic terms as follows:

- The global technology company's goal is to build a system level solution that is emission free and contributes to its vision of a 100% renewable energy future. Its role in the ecosystem is to provide the technological system that enables the conversion of electricity to hydrogen (Power-2-X, in this case X referring to hydrogen) and hydrogen to electricity (and other energy forms, i.e., X-2-Power).
- The energy company's goal is to provide CO_2 neutral energy production and support additional wind power investments. Its role in the ecosystem is to provide CO_2 neutral electricity for the system.
- The utility company's goal is to enable more flexibility into their energy system. It distributes the energy produced in the system to end-users. Its role is to use hydrogen for energy storage, allowing it to store the energy produced for when it is needed. In addition, the company utilises the heat from the production of hydrogen in the district heating network.
- The local city's goal is to advance its ambition of becoming CO_2 neutral before 2030. Its role is to support investments in CO_2 neutral infrastructure such as district heating or use of e-fuels.

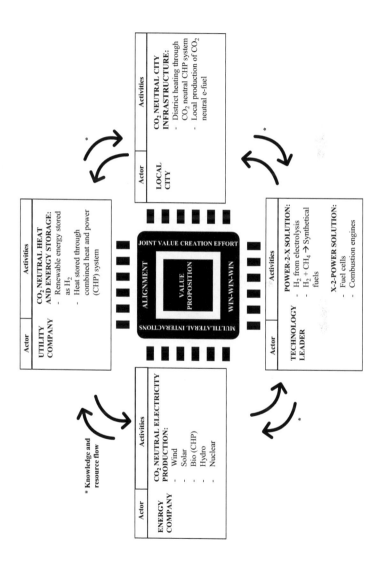

Figure 8.1 Model of ecosystem value proposition for production, usage, and storage of hydrogen. (H_2 = hydrogen, CO_2 = carbon dioxide, CHP = combined heat and power system, CH_4 = methane)

The partners came together around a common value proposition that concerns an ecosystem level solution for green hydrogen production, storage, and energy reconversion. It is an ecosystem level value proposition, where all actors find a win-win-win position. Through combining the complementary resources, activities and needs of the actors involved, all partners gain benefit. What makes this collaboration an ecosystem is that there is alignment between the partners and none of the actors can start providing solutions or utilising green hydrogen on their own. Specifically, for the value proposition to materialise, there are both compatible incentives and motives to participate in the joint value creation effort and complementarity in the configuration of activities among a defined set of partners who are multilaterally interacting (Adner, 2017).

By coming together around a common value proposition and having the set of relevant stakeholders (technological system provider for the hydrogen conversion, CO_2 neutral electricity producer, user of hydrogen for energy storage, and end customer for district heating), the partners can together create a solution that has the potential to be scaled up. However, building the needed infrastructure, industry standards, and economies of scale for realising the potential of scaling up this ecosystem value proposition will require the orchestration of activities of the different actors in a way that they simultaneously develop in the direction benefitting the collaboratively built value proposition.

Conclusion

Organising for sustainability in a way that can respond to the grand sustainability challenges of our time requires a shift in mindset from individual actors such as companies and other organisations to ecosystems. We argue that individual actors are not able to achieve substantive changes on their own, and an ecosystem approach to responsibility is needed to create partnerships (SDG 17) that can respond to the SDGs. The sense of urgency that both politicians and company decision-makers associate with responding to climate challenges has given momentum to an unprecedented willingness to invest both public and private resources in building new ecosystems that can offer sustainable solutions to tackle the multifaceted problems that we face today concerning climate, ecology, and a fairer society for all. The ecosystem approach offers a conceptual basis to rethink how different actors can interact and be aligned responsibly, so that system level change towards sustainability can be achieved. Thinking in terms of ecosystems and "win-win-win" requires overcoming deep-seated dominant paradigms of organising value creation. It also requires new practices that are based on trust, inclusion, and a shared vision of the goals for the future.

Acknowledgements

We acknowledge the financial support of the Academy of Finland (grant number: 322640).

References

Aarikka-Stenroos, L., & Ritala, P. (2017). Network management in the era of ecosystems: Systematic review and management framework. *Industrial Marketing Management*, *67*(April 2016), 23–36. https://doi.org/10.1016/j.indmarman.2017.08.010

Adner, R. (2017). Ecosystem as structure: An actionable construct for strategy. *Journal of Management*, *43*(1), 39–58. https://doi.org/10.1177/0149206316678451

European Commission (2020). *European Commission, communication from the Commission to the European Parliament, the Council, the European Economic and Social Committee and the Committee of the Regions: A hydrogen strategy for a climate-neutral Europe.* https://ec.europa.eu/energy/sites/ener/files/hydrogen_strategy.pdf

Hannah, D. P., & Eisenhardt, K. M. (2018). How firms navigate cooperation and competition in nascent ecosystems. *Strategic Management Journal*, (August 2017), 1–30. https://doi.org/10.1002/smj.2750

Jacobides, M. G., Cennamo, C., & Gawer, A. (2018). Towards a theory of ecosystems. *Strategic Management Journal*, *39*(8), 2255–2276. https://doi.org/10.1002/smj.2904

Jonker, J., Berkers, F., Derks, M., Montenegro Navarro, N., Wieclawska, S., Speijer, F., … Engels, H. (2020). *Collaborative business models for transition.* TNO, Den Haag. https://repository.tudelft.nl/ view/tno/uuid:7361e81d-ad35-4ed2-affb-a6baff36de24.

Nižetić, S., Barbir, F., & Djilali, N. (2021). The role of hydrogen in the energy transition. *Oxford Energy Forum*, *127*(May), 9673–9674. https://doi.org/10.1016/j.ijhydene.2019.02.174

Penttilä, K., Ravald, A., Dahl, J., & Björk, P. (2020). Managerial sensemaking in a transforming business ecosystem: Conditioning forces, moderating frames, and strategizing options. *Industrial Marketing Management*, *91*(May), 209–222. https://doi.org/10.1016/j.indmarman.2020.09.008

Rambhujun, N., Salman, M. S., Wang, T., Pratthana, C., Sapkota, P., Costalin, M., … Aguey-Zinsou, K.-F. (2020). Renewable hydrogen for

the chemical industry. *MRS Energy & Sustainability*, 7(1). https://doi.org/
10.1557/mre.2020.33

Walrave, B., Talmar, M., Podoynitsyna, K. S., Romme, A. G. L., & Verbong,
G. P. J. (2018). A multi-level perspective on innovation ecosystems for path-
breaking innovation. *Technological Forecasting and Social Change, 136*(April
2017), 103–113. https://doi.org/10.1016/j.techfore.2017.04.011

9 The (ir)responsibility of organisational innovation

Karl-Erik Sveiby and Beata Segercrantz

Introduction

This chapter explores (ir)responsible organising by analysing how academic researchers talk about negative consequences of organisational innovation (henceforth OI). Irresponsible organising refers here to OI practices through which managers try to secure their corporations' survival in the accelerating global competitive race, while giving little attention to how their solutions may affect stakeholders inside or outside the organisation. While the United Nations Sustainable Development Goals (SDGs) aim to foster innovation (SDG 9), its negative consequences are often ignored. We analyse how the irresponsibility of OI may hinder organising towards sustainable outcomes in organisations.

A serious shortcoming of the academic OI literature is its pro-innovation bias (Rogers, 2003, p. 436) that largely neglects negative consequences of innovation. Reviews have found that only 0.1–0.4 percent of innovation literature study these and that there is little change over the years (Rogers, 1983; Sveiby et al., 2012). To open up for alternative and more responsible paths for innovation, there is a need to challenge the dominant innovation approaches and discourses in the OI literature. Here OI studies could play a transformative role for responsible organising.

Reviewing organisational innovation literature

We conducted a systematic literature review (Tranfield, 2003) of negative consequences of OI in 288 journals and 12 academic books. We found a total of 146 papers, which we will refer to as ISNC (Innovation Studies of Negative Consequences; Godin & Vinck, 2017; Walsh, 2021). We analysed discursive constructions in the papers (interpretative

DOI: 10.4324/9781003229728-11

repertoires, subject positions, and ideological dilemmas) by drawing on critical discursive psychology. Interpretative repertoires are defined here as "relatively coherent ways of talking about objects and events in the world" (Edley, 2001, p. 198), i.e., available linguistic and social resources drawn upon by subjects when constructing particular versions of social reality (Potter & Wetherell, 1987). Subject positions refer to the ways in which subjects are positioned and position themselves within an interpretative repertoire (Davies & Harré, 1990). The concept ideological dilemma is used to discuss contradictory interpretative repertoires and/or subject positions (Billig et al., 1988).

Inspired by the crystallisation method (Ellingson, 2009) we constructed a narrative by interweaving verbatim quotes from the reviewed literature into a fictional story. The dominant themes in the reviewed literature are illustrated with quotes from 29 papers in our data set and structured as a story with a plot and actors. The narrative's references are available upon request from the first author.

A narrative of organisational innovation

In this section, we present our crystallised narrative, divided into six extracts with italicised citations representing dominant accounts from the studied literature.

Extract 1: The Board of the large European technology company T-Hy [fictional company] is pressured by competition and financial markets to *be more innovative* and *to improve its performance*. The CEO therefore implements an *organisational innovation* which will give a *strategic advantage*: a *sophisticated enterprise resource planning (ERP) system* delivered by a consultancy company, which will *standardise, integrate and automate the business processes*. Profitability increases and the company's share price rises.

Extract 2: The CEO is lauded in the financial press and most managers and employees are *enthusiastic about interacting directly with a computerised system* and new *opportunities and challenges*:

> *We had five systems that we consolidated into one system. I can now monitor risk from my desk more easily.*
> *I doubled my bonuses since we have this system.*

However, several factory employees become *unemployed due to technological change*.

Extract 3: The employees soon find that the *organisational innovation ERP intensifies the work pace and creates new tasks to complete, thus, requiring greater intensive and extensive efforts than before.* Managers complain about *increased demands on organisational attention:*

> *I did not anticipate the amount of time I had to spend making sure that the transition was smooth.*

Employees *accept* these consequences and are generally *satisfied*, because they are informed that research shows *labour-saving innovations can lead to gains in international competitiveness.* However, while the *accelerating pace of change* appears to *increase productivity* and to have *positive consequences* for employees, many feel *stress, anxiety, confusion, and reduced job satisfaction.*

Extract 4: The ERP system turns out to be highly complex and contains *latent errors* (dormant bugs, which appear long after the installation when stressed users operate the system in ways unforeseen by the IT-consultants). Soon, the first errors surface as *major adverse outcomes.* Unwittingly, the Board had become a victim of the *bandwagon effect.* An IT-consultancy executive recalls:

> *By the mid-1990s, ERP was a topic that was being bandied about in boardrooms. It wasn't just an IT-project, but a strategic business imperative ... every company needed to have an ERP implementation.*

Insufficient investment for *implementation and training, and poor design undermined productivity gains* and added more pain. The staff report undesirable *psychosocial factors at work,* such as *loss of control.*

T-Hy was stuck in the well-known *productivity paradox:* the failure of technology investments to increase productivity. The Board *was essentially living an illusion, though a self-chosen and – partly – self-constructed one.*

Extract 5: Some problems can be traced back to *contextual insensitivity by the consultancy* company hired to manage the ERP process. The problems will, however, never be traced back to the original ERP project, because T-Hy has more pressing issues: the early productivity gains, reported in financial media, had diffused the *technically inefficient innovation* like *a fashion* among their competitors and T-Hy's high-profile CEO is headhunted away. The Board thus turns its attention to recruiting a new CEO.

Extract 6: The new CEO presents his vision: *The future is ours to create!* It will be created by *a highly innovative strategy*: "To concentrate T-Hy on our unique strategic competencies, R&D and Brand Management." All production will be *outsourced to countries such as China and India* and products are only assembled at home. The implementation of the new vision makes half the workforce unemployed and is supported by an investment in a *Global Knowledge Management (KM) project*. The project *is a highly sophisticated intranet* to *facilitate knowledge sharing globally*.

> *The pilot enthused the participants* [IT-professionals]. *Emboldened, they became evangelists of intranet technology to their own divisions, who begin developing local versions that were not shared with developers in other divisions. Reinvention, then, was extremely common in an innovation initiative specifically aimed at preventing such reinvention.*

The KM system is terminated, and the experts become *deeply frustrated and disappointed because there was no sign for them, no appreciation at all for their tremendous work.*

The T-Hy executives now realise that the downsized company's remaining staff are *professionals* and the *company's most valuable resource*. They decide to become *a forerunner in IT and telecommunication* and implement *mobile technology* to *increase their productivity*. Some *teleworkers said such technology had made it easier for them to balance work and family*.

However, *as time passed, the majority of interviewees started considering it invasive and stressful*. Some of them required *treatment with psychotropic medications*, and drug consumption *with increased prescription rate in both the unemployed and those that had kept their jobs* was observed.

Negative consequences of organisational innovation

We identified three partly contradictory interpretative repertoires in the narrative that centre on "innovation driven productivity," "work intensification," and "unpredictability of technology implementation." These repertoires condition how OI is organised, contribute to unsustainable organisational practices and the subject positioning of different actors.

A central starting point in the reviewed literature is a conceptualisation of innovation as good for economy, business, and society (see also Godin & Vinck, 2017), demonstrated in Extract 1 of the narrative where T-Hy strives to enhance productivity by implementing an OI.

A strong optimistic evaluation of innovation offers an interpretative repertoire of "innovation-driven productivity" that sees OIs as a solution to improving performance.

The subject positions within this repertoire are constructed in Extract 2: the CEO is represented as a hero, while managers and employees are categorised as either enthusiastic or unemployed. This exemplifies how different groups of actors often are positioned in innovation studies. It is against the backdrop of the dominant interpretative repertoire of innovation driven productivity and the categorising of actors above that ISNC research is conducted, highlighting silenced effects of innovation management in OI studies.

In Extract 3, we see how innovation contributes to work intensification. Managers are surprised by the implementation's complexity. Many employees accept the changes, but over time experience more stress and dissatisfaction. ISNC draws attention to this issue by building an interpretative repertoire of "work intensification" and portraying actors in a contrasting way compared to subject positions (as enthusiastic and heroes) in relation to the innovation driven productivity repertoire.

ISNC also highlights other problematic effects. Extract 4 draws attention to latent errors that over time appear as bugs that disturb work. The implementation failed due to the decision-makers' faith in the innovative system's productivity gains and unattended latent errors. Examining this phenomenon, ISNC constructs an interpretative repertoire of "unpredictability of technology implementation." From this emerges a representation of decision-makers as disillusioned "management fashion followers" in an unsuccessful pursuit of productivity. Employees are portrayed as victims of the productivity paradox, struggling under pressure and loss of control.

How does T-Hy deal with the productivity paradox? As Extract 5 illustrates, T-Hy does not investigate the causes of the difficult situation the company finds itself in. Instead, another pressing concern becomes the Board's top priority, and a new chain of OI begins, as seen in Extract 6.

In Extract 6, a chain of OIs develops: outsourcing of production, implementation of a KM IT-system and teleworking supported by mobile technologies. The productivity paradox remains present as does the interpretative repertoires of innovation driven productivity, work intensification and the unpredictability of technology implementation. This may result in activities that generate innovation in an accelerating pace rather than producing reflection and dealing with the causes of negative consequences of innovation. This, in turn, may produce further negative consequences, failed projects, more frustration, dissatisfaction, and stress.

Conclusion

A central ideological dilemma can be identified in the narrative of OI: a contradiction between the repertoire of innovation driven productivity and the repertoires of work intensification and unpredictable technology implementation. Studies of OI typically build on the notion of innovation as an effective tool for improving productivity, thereby reinforcing instead of critically examining this dominant discourse. Individual companies, hence, have little or no help from the academic OI literature for responsible organising of innovation.

ISNC instead highlight irresponsible organising, with a never-ending demand for OI in organisations in their search for improved performance. Leaders are constructed as "management fashion followers" who create an internal climate of unpredictability while employees are positioned as subjects who transform from enthusiastic actors into stressed, frustrated, and dissatisfied employees or unemployed medication-using persons. Thus, ISNC provide accounts of OI and related technology as sources for work intensification and unpredictability, which may work against, rather than improve, productivity.

To conclude, it has not become easier for management to act responsibly. On the contrary, our discourse analysis suggests that organisations (1) are caught in an institutionalised ever-accelerating innovation race (Hasu et al., 2012) focused on productivity with little opportunity to reflect on or to deal with the dilemmas and (2) have no help from the pro-innovation biased OI literature. Only ISNC highlight the dark sides. In the quest for innovation (SDG 9), negative consequences on, for example, workers' health and well-being (SDG 3) and working environments (SDG 8) should not be ignored. If academic OI studies challenged the dominant innovation discourses and explored alternative and more responsible paths for OI, they could instead play a transformative role. This would contribute towards more responsible organising by drawing more attention to how to prevent or to reduce negative consequences of innovation. This could help management to increase the net positive effect of their efforts for society.

References

Billig, M., Condor, S., Edwards, D., Gane, M., Middleton, D., & Radley, A. (1988). *Ideological dilemmas: A social psychology of everyday thinking*. London: Sage.
Davies, B., & Harré, R. (1990). Positioning: The discursive production of selves. *Journal for the theory of social behaviour*, 20(1), 43–63. https://doi.org/10.1111/j.1468-5914.1990.tb00174.x

Edley, N. (2001). Analysing masculinity: Interpretative repertoires, ideological dilemmas and subject positions. M. Wetherell, S. Taylor, & S. J. Yates (Eds.), *Discourse as data: A guide for analysis* (pp.189–228). London: Sage.

Ellingson, L. L. 2009. *Engaging crystallization in qualitative research: An introduction.* Thousand Oaks: Sage Publications.

Godin, B., & Vinck, D. (Eds.). (2017). *Critical studies of innovation: Alternative approaches to the pro-innovation bias.* Cheltenham and Northampton, MA: Edward Elgar Publishing.

Hasu, M., Leitner, K., Solitander, N., & Varblane, U. (2012). Accelerating the innovation race. *Challenging the innovation paradigm, 9,* 87. New York, NY: Routledge.

Potter, J., & Wetherell, M. (1987). *Discourse and social psychology: Beyond attitudes and behaviour.* London: Sage.

Rogers, E. M. (1983; 2003). *Diffusion of innovations.* New York, NY: Free Press.

Sveiby, K. E. Gripenberg, P., & Segercrantz, B. (2012). *Challenging the innovation paradigm.* New York, NY: Routledge.

Tranfield, D., Denyer, D., & Smart, P. (2003). Towards a methodology for developing evidence-informed management knowledge by means of systematic review. *British journal of management, 14*(3), 207–222. https://doi.org/10.1111/1467-8551.00375

Walsh, S. (2021). Marx, subsumption and the critique of innovation. *Organization,* https://doi.org/10.1177/13505084211015377

References for the quotes in the narrative available from the first author upon request.

10 (Re)organising supply chains for responsibility

Anna Zhuravleva, Anna Aminoff, and David B. Grant

Introduction

This chapter discusses non-profit organisations (NPOs) that collect post-use textiles as donations from consumers. This is important because an average European Union consumer purchases about 26 kg and discards about 11 kg of textiles annually (European Environmental Agency, 2021). As a result, textiles do not last long, with an average lifecycle estimated to be about three years from the moment of purchase (Ekström & Salomonson, 2014). Such shortened lifecycles are caused by a dominant fast-fashion culture coupled with a throw-away attitude towards textile products among fashion consumers, which has led to a decline in product quality and durability (Brydges, 2021). The problem becomes what to do with used textiles that are unwanted or obsolete by consumers in the maturity or at the end of their lifecycle, also known as post-use textiles.

NPOs in many European countries have long been involved in collecting, sorting, and re-distributing post-use textiles. Post-use textiles are often considered as a single waste stream but actually have three streams: reusable, recyclable, and non-recyclable textiles (Nørup et al., 2018; Zhuravleva & Aminoff, 2021). This chapter discusses the sustainability of current supply chains for post-use textiles and the opportunities and challenges that forthcoming legislation for textile reuse and recycling is going to bring. The discussion gives insights on how to responsibly organise post-use textile supply chains so that they minimise textile waste and offer sustainable consumption alternatives (United Nations Sustainable Development Goal, SDG 12).

NPOs and reverse logistics processes for textile reuse

Not all textiles that are permanently discarded by consumers are at the end of their lifecycle. Some products can be still reused in their original

DOI: 10.4324/9781003229728-12

form, be repaired, or become source material for new products. Reuse is one of the most environmentally friendly lifecycle management strategies that saves resources invested in production and prevents the generation of waste. At the EU-level reuse has been given a strategic priority before recycling and incineration and emphasised in the EU Directive on waste (Official Journal of the European Union, 2018). For textile consumers, reuse is a rather old and familiar practice. For example, clothing is exchanged between family and friends, sold or given away through flea markets or online, or donated to NPOs, who are the largest collectors of waste textiles (Pal, 2017). Oxfam, Red Cross, Texaid, and UFF are a few of the NPOs that organise collection of post-use textiles donated from consumers and sell them through their own networks of charity shops and distribution partners (Nørup et al., 2019; Pal, 2017).

Reverse logistics processes (collection and sorting) are an important factor to ensure donation inflow from consumers (Pal, 2017; Paras et al., 2018). NPOs compete to obtain high quality donations of post-use textiles between each other and with other actors, such as communal waste management companies and private second-hand companies. To get the donations, NPOs arrange their collection systems to be close-to-donor and the most convenient for consumers. For example, consumers can leave donations at a static container, use pick-up services provided by NPOs or their logistics partners, or make direct donations to a collection point at the charity shop.

Collected donations are manually sorted into a range of categories by quality levels, functionality, gender, and seasonality in sorting centres (Nørup et al., 2018). At this point, textile design and brand play a major role in product success in the secondary market (Paras et al., 2018). Luxury branded clothing, for example, has high potential for reuse even if the textile product itself has minor defects. A special category of post-use textiles is vintage selection. Workers on the sorting line often receive special training on recognising valuable pieces from the past that could satisfy the taste of fashion consumers of today. Studies highlight that the training and professional education related to textile or fashion are the factors that define and improve efficiency in the sorting process and, as a result, increase the reuse potential (Beh et al., 2016; Pal, 2017).

(Re)organising for sustainable textile reuse

NPOs differ in their objectives and strategies with some emphasising ecologically sustainable aspects of their work while others emphasise the societally sustainable impact they are trying to achieve through textile reuse. For example, the European organisation Texaid is a private partnership charity with a strong environmental and business focus. Texaid collects used textiles primarily via collection containers, sorts them in centralised sorting facilities, and runs their own reuse and recycling activities. For example, in Germany, its largest area of operations, it has around 50 second-hand shops. Texaid offers solutions for retailers that cover overstock, online returns, off-season inventories, and logo removing services. The organisation also specialises in the production of cleaning cloths, recycled wool, and mechanically shredded raw material for insulation and roofing felts.

The Finnish Red Cross (FRC) is a significantly different organisation. FRC operates its textile collection primarily in-store with support from a few collection containers. Besides the second-hand charity shops, humanitarian clothing aid is one of the equally important collection purposes. According to the principles of the Red Cross, clothing aid is sent upon a request from a local Red Cross unit. The clothing is carefully checked and categorised by gender, functionality, and seasonality. In the sorting process, the organisation checks clothing for sensitive content (for example, prints with weapons or inappropriate images), respect to local traditions (for example, longer skirts for women), and specifics of material (no fur products to avoid bugs in long-term transportation). In recent years, Mongolia has been the target country of one of the longest clothing aid projects for FRC.

The problem of post-use textile exports

A potential problem with the current supply chain for post-use textiles is post-use textile exports. For example, UFF, the largest collector of post-use textiles in Finland, collects around 15 million tons of textiles annually, but after the sorting process, only about 3–4% of the post-use textiles qualify for charity shops in Finland with most donations exported to the Baltic countries through the partner network. The textiles are then distributed further with a low transparency of their journey and ultimate destination.

Post-use textile export exists for several reasons. First, the export of used textiles is an activity that brings NPOs additional monetary funds for their global development work along with the second-hand charity shops and helps keep them economically viable. Second, the sorting facilities located in the Baltic countries have larger processing capacity and lower labour costs than Finland. For example, a textile sorting centre of the Humana People to People Federation (UFF is a part of this Federation) in Lithuania has a daily processing capacity of 200 tons per day with a daily average of 130 tons (Nørup et al., 2019).

Lastly, NPOs have few opportunities to find domestic use for lower-quality textiles due to a lack of scalable domestic solutions for textile recycling. The potential for recycling is still not fully realised due to a lack of technology, for example, in sorting collected textiles, working with fibre blends, and separating fibres from chemicals (CBI, 2021).

The problem arises when post-use textiles end up in developing countries where they have a negative impact on the socio-economic development of these countries. Imported post-use textiles become a harmful substitute for locally produced textile items and reinforce societal issues such as poverty (SDG 1) and inequality (SDG 10; Brooks and Simon, 2012). Indeed, in recent years NPOs have increased their export of post-use textiles from the country of collection (Nørup et al., 2019) and independent studies have proved that lower-quality pieces donated to NPOs can end up in developing countries (Yle, 2020).

Introducing legislation for post-use textile management

The position of NPOs and their textile collection activities might experience a change with the introduction of new legislation related to textile waste. Recently, the EU has introduced a Directive on waste that obliges all EU member states to establish separate collection of post-use textiles by the year 2025 (European Environmental Agency, 2021). Besides this regulatory pressure, the development of sustainable solutions for post-use textile management has also been driven by new business potential with recycled textiles as well as ecological concerns (Zhuravleva & Aminoff, 2021). In practice, such a collection system targets textile recycling, and the EU member states must ensure that post-use textiles are collected as a separate waste fraction and sorted into different categories for textile reuse, recycling, and incineration. For example, Finland aims at establishing a national separate collection system for post-use textiles and launch a textile processing factory by the year 2023 (LSJH, 2020).

The forthcoming EU legislation is likely to disrupt the current supply chains for textile reuse. It is an opportunity to valorise post-use textiles domestically and thus, reduce international exports. A potential issue for NPOs' own collection is related to the consumers' subjective perceptions of (re)usability that would see reusable textiles appear in the wrong collection system. Another aspect, previously mentioned, is the convenience and proximity of the collection points. If the national collection system for textile recycling will be closer to the end consumer, NPOs might experience a decline in donation inflows. If NPOs partner with the collection system network, sorting of post-use textiles for domestic recycling can potentially lead to additional logistics costs for NPOs or confuse textile donors about the NPO's collection goals and decrease the quality of collected textiles (Zhuravleva & Aminoff, 2021).

However, forthcoming legislation can initiate a reorganisation of the supply chain for post-use textiles, improving its sustainability. This would require new partnerships and links between the NPOs and networks of partners in the collection system. The experience of NPOs is valuable for initiatives related to implementation of the EU Directive on waste and inclusion of NPOs in discussions about the domestic collection system for post-use textiles has a strategic importance (Zhuravleva & Aminoff, 2021). The charitable cause of NPOs' collection is a strong incentive for textile donors to bring their textiles for reuse; thus, NPOs can become a reuse-oriented actor fulfilling this new EU legislation.

Conclusion

The activities of NPOs for textile reuse support the United Nations' Agenda 2030 and its SDGs in several ways. First, NPOs provide an ecological alternative for textile consumers (SDG 12). In addition, these organisations support environmental initiatives to avoid textile waste and collect textiles for valorisation purposes (SDG 13). Finally, NPOs can influence many other SDGs with funds generated through textile reuse as their development work addresses but is not limited to the reduction of poverty, hunger, and inequalities (SDGs 1, 2, 10). Securing a niche for this type of actor in textile reuse and recycling is important when (re)organising responsibly for sustainable outcomes in the textile industry.

Acknowledgements

This work was supported by the Foundation for Economic Education in Finland.

References

Beh, L. S., Ghobadian, A., He, Q., Gallear, D., & O'Regan, N. (2016). Second-life retailing: a reverse supply chain perspective. *Supply Chain Management*, 21(2), 259–272. https://doi.org/10.1108/SCM-07-2015-0296

Brooks, A. & Simon, D. (2012). Unravelling the relationships between used-clothing imports and the decline of African clothing industries. *Development and Change*, 43(6), 1265–1290. https://doi.org/1111/j.1467-7660.2012.01797.x

Brydges, T. (2021). Closing the loop on take, make, waste: investigating circular economy practices in the Swedish fashion industry. *Journal of Cleaner Production*, 293, 126–245. https://doi.org/10.1016/j.jclepro.2021.126245

CBI. (2021). The European market potential for recycled fashion. Retrieved from: www.cbi.eu/market-information/apparel/recycled-fashion/market-potential (Accessed 28 September 2021)

Ekström, K M. & Salomonson, N. (2014). Reuse and recycling of clothing and textiles: a network approach. *Journal of Macromarketing*, 34(3), 383–399. https://doi.org/10.1177/0276146714529658

European Environmental Agency. (2021). Textiles in Europe's circular economy. Retrieved from: www.eea.europa.eu/publications/textiles-in-europes-circular-economy (Accessed 28 September 2021)

LSJH. (2020). Nordic countries' first large-scale end-of-life textile refinement plant to open in Paimio in 2021. Retrieved from: www.lsjh.fi/en/nordic-countries-first-large-scale-end-of-life-textile-refinement-plant-to-open-in-paimio-in-2021/ (Accessed 28 September 2021)

Nørup, N., Pihl, K., Damgaard, A. & Scheutz, C. (2018). Development and testing of a sorting and quality assessment method for textile waste. *Waste Management*, 79, 8–21. https://doi.org/10.1016/j.wasman.2018.07.008

Nørup, N., Pihl, K., Damgaard, A. & Scheutz, C. (2019). Evaluation of a European textile sorting centre: material flow analysis and life cycle inventory. *Resources, Conservation and Recycling*, 143, 310–319. https://doi.org/10.1016/j.resconrec.2019.01.010

Official Journal of the European Union. (2018). Directive (EU) 2018/851 of the European Parliament and of the Council of 30 May 2018 amending Directive 2008/98/EC on waste. Retrieved from: https://eur-lex.europa.eu/legal-content/EN/TXT/?uri=uriserv:OJ.L_.2018.150.01.0109.01.ENG (Accessed 28 September 2021)

Pal, R. (2017). Value creation through reverse logistics in used clothing networks. *The International Journal of Logistics Management*, 28(3), 864–906. https://doi.org/10.1108/IJLM-11-2016-0272

Paras, M. K., Ekwall, D., Pal, R., Curteza, A., Chen, Y. & Wang, L. (2018). An exploratory study of Swedish charities to develop a model for the reuse-based clothing value chain. *Sustainability*, 10(4). https://doi.org/10.3390/su10041176

Yle. (2020). Keräyslatikosta kansainväliseksi kauppatavaraksi. Minne vanha vaateesi päättyy? Retrieved from: https://yle.fi/aihe/artikkeli/2020/02/17/mot-laittoi-lahettimia-kierratysvaatteisiin-nain-lahjoittamasi-vaatteet (Accessed 28 September 2021)

Zhuravleva, A. & Aminoff, A. (2021). Emerging partnerships between non-profit organizations and companies in reverse supply chains: enabling valorization of post-use textile. *International Journal of Physical Distribution & Logistics Management*, 51(9), 978–998. https://doi.org/10.1108/IJPDLM-12-2020-0410

11 Responsible markets and marketing

*Meri-Maaria Frig, Pia Polsa, and
Jonna Heliskoski*

Introduction

This chapter argues that the traditional logic of markets and marketing, and their underlying assumption of shareholder wealth accumulation, is irresponsible, and offers ideas for a reversal of logic. Markets and marketing have long been studied mainly from the economic point of view and with the logic of economic organising to create shareholder value and wealth. However, markets and marketing are also known to have a powerful, destructive influence on our societies and beyond. To change this, the logic of markets and marketing need to be reversed from the purely economic rational to a more responsible one.

Complex and constantly changing markets of goods and services (online and offline) shape and challenge the way we organise our economies and societies. In this chapter, we illustrate how markets and marketing shape what we desire in terms of, for example, "good health and well-being" (United Nations Sustainable Development Goal, SDG 3) and "decent work and economic growth" (SDG 8) and how our actions influence "responsible consumption and production" (SDG 12).

We show how important it is that both consumers and producers (SDG 12) partner with non-economic actors (SDG 17), not only to reach the SDGs, but to understand, acknowledge, and act upon responsibility. We draw on macromarketing and social marketing research to demonstrate how market actors have made efforts to change society and challenge the unsustainable consumerist culture. However, none of these efforts and movements have been able to reverse mainstream economic logic. There is an urgent need to change the logic towards responsible shaping of markets and responsible organising of marketing.

DOI: 10.4324/9781003229728-13

Reversing the logic of marketing

Consumption in the modern economy is increasingly prominently linked to social and environmental impact (Johnston, 2008). At the same time, research shows how present levels of consumption put increasing pressure on the limits of the Earth's ecosystems. Marketing has played a key role in inducing consumerism. Marketing is commonly defined as "the activity, set of institutions, and processes for creating, communicating, delivering, and exchanging offerings that have value for customers, clients, partners, and society at large" (AMA, 2017). Although ethical consumption has received attention in both research and public discourse, the actual share of consumers that make consumption decisions based on ethico-moral considerations has remained low (Carrington et al., 2016).

The idea that a sovereign consumer driven by self-interest has the power to change society towards a sustainable future is argued to be an illusion that primarily distorts attention away from the unsustainability and destructiveness of consumerist capitalism (Carrington et al., 2016; Cherrier & Murray, 2004). Radical changes are required (Sandberg, 2021) beyond economic goals towards reversing the logic of marketing.

In response to current sustainability challenges, as demonstrated by the 17 SDGs, marketing scholars have started to investigate the role and responsibility of market actors *in and as part of* society. Markets and marketing can no longer be examined as separate from other spheres of society (Layton & Grossbart, 2006) or the natural environment (Kotler, 2011). For example, scholars have asked whether capitalism can create solutions to the environmental, social, and economic destruction that it has brought about (Carrington et al., 2016), or whether solutions need to be found from movements that challenge capitalist modes of production and consumption (Bonsu & Polsa, 2011). Market actors must now listen to multiple voices: not only of human stakeholders, but of ecosystems, animals, and future generations.

If traditional marketing has shaped consumer behaviour and markets towards unsustainability, then can a reverse logic in marketing shape them towards responsibility? Since the 1970s, the scholarly fields of social marketing and macromarketing have worked for such reversal. The purpose of social marketing is "to transform society for the greater good" (Saunders et al., 2015, p. 165), while macromarketing is defined as "the study of (1) marketing systems, (2) the impact and consequence of marketing systems on society, and (3) the impact and consequence of society on marketing systems" (Hunt, 1981, p. 8). Social marketing and macromarketing show potential to reverse the logic of markets and marketing from one of excessive consumption to one of sustainability. When social marketing is combined with macromarketing we can address complex and interconnected problems at several levels of society: macro, meso, and micro (Kennedy et al., 2017).

When investigating markets and marketing from a systems perspective (Kadirov, 2018), the individual consumer is not the central actor, as in traditional marketing theory. From a systems perspective, choices of consumers as well as companies are enabled and restricted by structural forces such as media, policy and regulations, culture and advertising, globalisation, and primacy of shareholder value (Carrington et al., 2016; Cherrier & Murray, 2004). Hence, a multilevel perspective addressing the macro, meso, and micro levels is needed.

Investigating markets and marketing from a systems perspective, we can ask, what drives change in current societies (Kadirov, 2018)? We suggest two primary ways that enable market disruptions and make change happen. First, market actors can enable and influence purposeful collective action by appealing to others with aligned values (Kadirov, 2018). Second, market actors, together or individually, can challenge existing institutions to facilitate societal change (Klein, 2017; Thompson & Coskuner-Balli, 2007). The following section presents three examples of how this can be achieved in practice.

Markets and marketing for sustainable outcomes

Shaping markets: business models to alleviate poverty

In the 1990s Prahalad and Lieberthal (1998) published their seminal work on how to integrate the world's poorest, the "Bottom-of-the-Pyramid" (BoP), into the global capitalist system. The core idea was to integrate the poor as consumers of Western oriented business models. Companies like Tikau in India (https://tikau.com) and Mifuko in Kenya (https://mifuko.com) have turned this idea around by arguing that the way to decrease poverty (SDG 1) and enhance social well-being is to acknowledge the Indigenous designs and skills among the vulnerable and provide livelihood (SDG 8) by buying from the less affluent rather than selling to them. The business model of both companies is to find artefacts and handicraft skills in countries like Kenya and India, design products that fit the taste of affluent countries, brand the products, and sell them at a price that gives the original producers a decent income (SDG 12).

Rather than attempting to maximise the profit of the company, as traditional marketing logic would suggest, Tikau and Mifuko challenge traditional business models and reverse the logic, focusing on increasing well-being in the sourcing communities in India and Kenya. Business model innovations such as these in the Global South challenge existing ways of doing business and can shape markets to become more sustainable. Examples such as Tikau and Mifuko show that BoP business models can be profitable, sustainable and well-being enhancing exercises. However, one must caution against the risk of falling into "corporate saviourism" (see Chapter 13).

Marketing for increased well-being: working with different but compatible sales arguments

The Ministry of Social Affairs and Health in Finland in the Global North has funded several projects focusing on preventive strategies for health (SDG 3), such as "Strength in Old Age" (www.voimaavanhuuteen.fi/en/) and "Neuvokas perhe" ("resourceful family"; https://neuvokasperhe.fi/en/). Social marketing and an analysis of customer value on different levels of observation helped to bring the projects forward.

The challenge with both projects was that they had at least three target audiences, which they intended to impact:

- Micro: end-customers and beneficiaries (elderly and family).
- Meso: healthcare workers in the organisations that would implement the project.
- Macro: municipalities who would finance the project.

For each audience, the argument to adapt the project was different because the customer profile was different. For the final beneficiaries, who in both cases were vulnerable individuals, the initial sales argument was the health benefits of preventive actions. However, preventive actions as such were not marketable for this audience. More sellable value proposals were fun and social interaction, and these became the message that social marketing helped to frame. Healthcare workers who were needed to implement the programmes, in turn, could not always be attracted by altruistic ideas such as the well-being of the vulnerable. The sales argument for them was to ease their workload when both families and elderly take preventive actions. Municipalities needed to get involved to fund the projects. The value proposal for them was purely economic: investing in preventive programmes served to reduce future costs.

Implementation of both programmes was successful due to social marketing being implemented at three levels (micro, meso, macro), creating separate but compatible sales arguments at each level. The projects applied tools from macromarketing and social marketing. The example shows how marketing logics can be challenged and reversed by using tools from marketing, traditionally used for profit maximisation, to achieve positive social outcomes.

Harnessing marketing channels for sustainability: the potential of influencers

Social media influencers often initiate unexpected critical conversations about corporate legitimacy. For example, in summer 2021, the Finnish blogger Annamari Värtö wrote a post on her blog about the harmful impacts of mosquito repellents. In her blog and social media posts, Värtö drew attention to the device's effects on ecosystems and biodiversity (SDG 15), as its active ingredients are known to be highly toxic to aquatic organisms and pollinators. As the blog post gained increasing attention in social media, two retailers pulled the product from their shelves until further information about the product's safety will become available. In June 2021, a member of the European parliament submitted a written question, asking for an assessment of the active substances used in mosquito repellent devices, to possibly ban their sale (European Parliament, 2021).

This exemplifies how different actors can rapidly influence market systems by influencing the general opinion and local consumption culture, to the extent of potentially changing legislation. A number of market actors from different spheres of society (e.g., social media influencers and politicians) acted collectively to address the use of potentially unsafe mosquito repellents.

Social media influencers are today regarded as critical actors to society when information needs to be disseminated to a variety of audiences. For example, at the peak of the COVID-19 crisis, in March 2020, the Finnish government officially classified social media influencers as critical operators, and through a social media consultancy, worked together with over a thousand influencers to communicate fact-based information about the crisis (SDG 3).

Marketing channels, such as social media, can be harnessed for marketing sustainability, in contrast to their traditional focus on inducing consumerism and endorsing harmful industries. They can be used to increase understanding of human connections to current environmental and social crises, including in partnership with commercial and other actors. Actors such as social media influencers can challenge current norms and institutions and, as in the case of the mosquito repellent, initiate collective action for sustainable outcomes.

Conclusion

This chapter has shown how the logic of markets and marketing can be reversed from a purely economic rational to a responsible one that would create value for individuals, societies, and our common planet and transform marketing from unsustainable actions to responsible organising. Our different examples demonstrate that transformative marketing initiatives include partnerships between several actors (SDG 17) and require a deeper understanding of markets, the business-society relationship, and the needs and desires of individuals and future generations.

Our first example shows how existing market institutions can be challenged through business model innovations that place creation of well-being above economic value creation. Our second example shows how tools from marketing – in particular, combining macromarketing and social marketing – can be used for sustainable outcomes rather than profit maximisation. Our third example illustrates how both individual advocates (such as influencers) and established institutions (political decision-makers and the state) can leverage marketing channels such as social media to transmit critical information regarding the environment and society and influence purposeful collective action towards sustainable outcomes. While we have provided individual examples of responsible marketing, more concerted efforts are needed to reverse the logic of markets and marketing.

Acknowledgements

We wish to acknowledge the financial support we received from the CORE project (www.collaboration.fi/) funded by the Strategic Research Council at the Academy of Finland (grant number: 313017).

References

AMA (2017). Definitions of marketing. www.ama.org/the-definition-of-marketing/
Bonsu, S. & Polsa, P. (2011). Governmentality at the 'Base-of-the Pyramid'. *Journal of Macromarketing*, 31(3), 236–244. https://doi.org/10.1177/0276146711407506
Carrington, M. J., Zwick, D. & Neville, B. (2016). The ideology of the ethical consumption gap. *Marketing Theory*, 16(1), 21–38. https://doi.org/10.1177/1470593115595674
Cherrier, H. & Murray, J. B. (2004). The sociology of consumption: the hidden facet of marketing. *Journal of Marketing Management*, 20(5–6), 509–525. https://doi.org/10.1362/0267257041323954
European Parliament. (2021). *Subject: environmental effects of mosquito repellent devices*. 23 June 2021. www.europarl.europa.eu/doceo/document/E-9-2021-003270_EN.html

Hunt, S. (1981). Macromarketing as a multidimensional concept. *Journal of Macromarketing*, 1(1), 7–8. https://doi.org/10.1177/027614678100100103

Johnston, J. (2008). The citizen-consumer hybrid: ideological tensions and the case of whole foods market. *Theory and Society,* 37(3), 229–270. https://doi.org/10.1007/s11186-007-9058-5

Kadirov, D. (2018). Towards a theory of marketing systems as the public good. *Journal of Macromarketing*, 38(3), 278–297. https://doi.org/10.1177/0276146718767949

Kennedy, A-M., Kapitan, S., Bajaj, N., Bakonyi, A. & Sands, S. (2017). Uncovering wicked problem's system structure: seeing the forest from the trees. *Journal of Social Marketing*, 7(1), 51–73. https://doi.org/10.1108/JSOCM-05-2016-0029

Klein, N. (2017). *No is not enough: resisting Trump's shock politics and winning the world we need.* Chicago, IL: Haymarket Books.

Kotler, P. (2011). Reinventing marketing to manage the environmental imperative. *Journal of Marketing*, 75(4), 132–135. https://doi.org/10.1509/jmkg.75.4.132

Layton, R. A. & Grossbart, S. (2006). Macromarketing: past, present, and possible future. *Journal of Macromarketing*, 26(2), 193–213. https://doi.org/10.1177/0276146706294026

Prahalad, C. K. & Lieberthal, K. (1998). The end of corporate imperialism. *Harvard Business Review*, 76 (4), 68–79.

Sandberg, M. (2021). Sufficiency transitions: a review of consumption changes for environmental sustainability. *Journal of Cleaner Production*, 293, 1–16. https://doi.org/10.1016/j.jclepro.2021.126097

Saunders, S. G., Barrington, D. J. and Sridharan, S. (2015). Redefining social marketing: beyond behavioural change. *Journal of Social Marketing*, 5(2), 160–168. https://doi.org/10.1108/JSOCM-03-2014-0021

Thompson, C. J. & Coskuner-Balli, G. (2007). Countervailing market responses to corporate co-optation and the ideological recruitment of consumption communities. *Journal of Consumer Research*, 34(2), 135–152. https://doi.org/10.1086/519143

Part III
Challenging inequalities

12 The logistification of humanitarian relief

Nikodemus Solitander and Eija Meriläinen

Introduction

This chapter explores the organisation of humanitarian relief *through*, and *as*, global supply chains, referred to as logistification of humanitarian relief (LHR). The aim of humanitarian relief is to support crisis-affected people in meeting their needs, an activity that increasingly revolves around the organisation of supply chains. Contemporary humanitarian relief comprises organising of flows of commodities (e.g., food), money (e.g., cash-based assistance), financialised instruments (e.g., vaccine bonds), and data (e.g., tracking information). We argue that this rapid growth of "logistification" serves to upkeep a politics of Empire, past and present. Empire here refers to the apparatus, constructed by nations and actors of the "centre," for exploiting the labour and resources from locations subjugated as the "periphery" (Hardt & Negri, 2000).

The logistification of humanitarianism adds a layer of tension in balancing between the increasingly blurred boundaries of complex emergencies and chronic vulnerabilities (Pascucci, 2021). Logistification entails more than an increased focus on the organisation of material flows and transportation – it subjugates humanitarian relief to global supply chains of Empire (Suwandi, 2019). Scrutinising the entanglements of LHR with Empire exposes not only the business logics at the heart of contemporary humanitarian relief (c.f. Attewell, 2018), but also asks what forms of humanitarianism are naturalised and opens for new imaginations of organising humanitarian relief.

The chapter identifies three patterns of LHR and its organisation in and through global supply chains: (1) The increased dominance of post-politics, (2) The interplay between bio- and necropolitics, and (3) The expansion of calculative logics. The patterns are illustrated with examples of how they serve to upkeep centre-periphery dynamics in

DOI: 10.4324/9781003229728-15

Haiti. The chapter shows how the organisation of humanitarian relief maintains unequal relations in the world-system, particularly among countries (United Nations Sustainable Development Goal, SDG 10), making visible the (ir)responsibilities associated with logistified humanitarianism.

Three patterns in the logistification of humanitarian relief

While the face of Empire has changed since early colonialism, transportation – or the supply chain – is still its lifeline. The supply chain is increasingly dominated by multinational corporations that extract surplus value from spatially dispersed sites. Each link in the global supply chain is expected to transfer value towards the centre (Suwandi, 2019). Organising global supply chains is thus central to maintaining the unequal exchange and imperial hierarchies between centre and periphery (Cowen, 2014).

The pursuit of humanitarianism is "the attempt to relieve the suffering of distant strangers" (Barnett, 2014, p. 243). While a humanitarian supply chain is typically organised identically to its commercial counterparts, the two differ in their supposed ends: "... business logistics aims at increasing profits whereas humanitarian logistics aims at alleviating the suffering of vulnerable people" (Kovacs & Spens, 2007, p. 107). The ends, however, cannot be untangled from the means. Humanitarian relief, while geared towards addressing supposedly sudden events rather than long-term developments, forms one part of the development (aid) complex that serves to give a human(itarian) face to Empire. In the case of a crisis, humanitarian relief momentarily appears to give back from the centre towards the peripheries but without altering the power hierarchies. We posit that the relationships between oppressors and oppressed are negotiated through the language of humanitarianism (Skinner & Lester, 2012). In the following sections we identify three patterns of this language.

The post-politics of humanitarian relief

The first pattern associated with LHR relates to the "post-political meaning that all problems are to be dealt with through administrative-organisational-technical means" (Swyngedouw, 2011, p. 373). In contrast, politics arises when particular groups demand "to be included in the public sphere, to be heard on equal footing with ruling oligarchy or aristocracy" (Žižek, 2006, p. 69). Modern humanitarianism discourse can be divided into two strands. The first one builds on a post-political, technical rational and a "hands off attitude towards politics" (Barnett, 2014, p. 243), creating a humanitarian space that attaches itself to ethics while segregating itself from politics. Logistification feeds the appearance of being able to organise humanitarian relief without politics. The second strand, largely ignored in LHR, treats politics as a necessary part of relief action, while also targeting the root causes of suffering (ibid).

Post-politics serves to silence questioning of unequal exchange between the centre and the periphery, and its social relations. In addition, it reduces the crisis-affected person into an apolitical and passive "beneficiary" (Barnett, 2014). This is not to say humanitarian relief workers are oblivious of the struggle between domination and emancipation (Barnett, 2014), but these aspects are not deemed "technical" or "managerial" and are thus left outside of the realm of possible action. Yet when combined with attempts in global supply chains to repress dissent of exploited workers (Suwandi, 2019), it can result in subduing of community organising (Ferguson, 1994).

The bio- and necropolitics of humanitarian relief

The second pattern associated with the LHR involves an interplay and constant ebb and flow between biopolitics and necropolitics (Fassin, 2007). Biopolitics refers to the regimes of power that regulate populations and administering life by targeting their biological attributes (ibid), such as the determination of "basic needs" for physical survival. Necropolitics is the subjugation of life to the power of death, i.e., capacities to decide who is disposable, exposing people to the *possibility* of death (Mbembe, 2003 in Attewell, 2018). The biopolitics of LHR has historically been tethered to a necropolitics of violence, with global supply chains both products of and prerequisite for death/violence (Attewell, 2018). This is visible in, for example, how military power straddles simultaneously the life-sustaining and life-eliminating flows in the humanitarian supply chains. Both organised forms of humanitarian relief (Skinner & Lester, 2012) and business logistics (Cowen, 2014) have strong military roots, associated with Empire. Humanitarianism, business, and military logics continue to have mutually reinforcing roles, as "militaries and logistics firms serve as humanitarians, and humanitarianism helps to expand and grow military power and commercial reach" (Ziadah, 2019, p. 1696).

Humanitarianism is often understood as an unmediated gesture of human connection to meet the needs of crisis-affected people (Barnett, 2014). However, the militarised supply chain can shift focus from the needs of humans to securing supply. LHR plays an important role in maintaining Empire, its effectiveness stemming from the organising of the ebb and flow of biopolitics of survival and necropolitics of subjugation of life to the power of death, often through the same hypersecuritised supply chains.

Expansion of calculative logics in humanitarian relief

The third pattern associated with LHR is the expansion of calculative logics into humanitarianism (Pascucci, 2021). Humanitarian relief has grown into an industry and been "professionalised" (ibid), increasingly drawing on business logics, with business school graduates governing the operations. Logistification actively contributes to this shift. Logistics is concerned with attempts to speed up the turnover time of capital (Suwandi, 2019), with overt focus on supply chain efficiency. The calculative logics associated with frameworks such as Just in Time Delivery, return on (donor) investment, quantitative cost modelling, and the privatisation of service delivery, have become key praxis of humanitarian relief (Ziadah, 2019). These calculative logics are reflected in how human needs are converted to cost-benefit analyses as well as in quantified minimum standard practices, such as the global Sphere standards for humanitarian action (https://spherestandards.org/).

Measures of accountability impose their own calculative logics to control the relief supply chains. This means that, as transparency masquerades as accountability, various technical proxies and intermediaries – such as standards based on calculative logics or experts in such logics, such as rating agencies and accountants – are inserted into the supply chain between the centre and the periphery. While this may increase accountability narrowly defined, it also contributes to what can be labelled as a relief from responsibility, when actors are enabled to distance themselves from responsibility by denial of proximity between relevant stakeholders in the supply chain. This creates situations where humanitarian supply chains serve to increase the spatial division between logisticians who are managing the supply chain at a distance, the aid workers in the field, the manual labourers in the supply chain, and those populations affected both by the crises and the effects of organised humanitarian relief (Ziadah, 2019).

Organising humanitarian relief in Haiti

When Haiti was struck by a heavy earthquake in 2010, the resulting crisis had a long history with Empire. Both France and the USA have treated

Haiti as their colonial periphery, giving shape to its vulnerabilities. In 2010, the US military operated in Haiti without appropriate mandate, the Haitian parliament dissolved itself under pressure from UN donors and was governed by the Interim Haiti Reconstruction Commission, co-chaired by former US president Bill Clinton, while various Western non-governmental organisations (NGOs) started flooding in (Schuller, 2016). The (post)colonial history is ever-present in Haiti, but as we will argue, the imperial patterns left in the wake of humanitarian relief create particular relations between actors in the relief chain.

First, the post-political nature of humanitarian supply chains in Haiti is striking. The island has for decades been referred to as an "NGO republic," reaching its epitome through the 2010 earthquake when government functions were given to private (Western) NGOs to ensure "oversight and accountability" in the rebuilding process (Schuller, 2016). The post-political condition of LHR became increasingly visible through the inserting of an "audit mentality." In Haiti, international NGOs explicitly avoided working with any local organisation whose audits revealed any activity deemed as political. The reasoning was that this would limit political opportunism and corruption – but in doing so actively sought to depoliticise local organisations, which in turn created a decoupling of economic development from political action (Vannier, 2010).

Second, border spaces between the USA and Haiti are also scene for the constant ebb and flow of biopolitics and necropolitics in humanitarian relief chains. Military-backed US humanitarian relief organisations have made sure the relief that can address "basic needs" reaches its selected targets through securitised supply chains to Haiti, underscoring the biopolitics of sustaining life. Meanwhile, at its own borders (and in Haiti), through necropolitics of military power and violence, the USA controls who becomes a "migrant" or "refugee," who can enter the USA, who are to stay in Haiti, and who are "illegal immigrants," "securely" delivered back to Haiti or placed in refugee camps through various securitised flows of bodies in a supply chain. The flow of refugees between Haiti and the USA shows how deployment of military force in humanitarian relief reinforces immobility regimes between the centre and the periphery, with enhanced border controls, migrant interdiction, and criminalisation often targeting marginalised and racialised populations.

Third, calculative logics of supplying humanitarian relief are visible in the politics of housing following the 2010 Haiti earthquake, which failed to address the crisis-affected people's need for a home. Notions of family in the Caribbean centre around solidarity and a multigenerational family form (Schuller, 2016). In the aftermath of the earthquake, many who had lost their homes had to rely on NGOs' tarps and camp management to access housing. Schuller (2016) describes an example of a camp where identical tents were pitched up for various types of families. Whilst this was "obviously done because of efficiency and deploying humanitarian knowledge about emergency shelter construction methods" (p. 86), this pushed for splitting up families and encouraged small family units, ignoring the needs and lives of the local communities. This contributed to breaking the networks of solidarity and support at the moment when they would be most needed.

Conclusion

The chapter has discussed patterns of LHR that forge the relations between actors in global supply chains. These patterns reveal the maintenance of unequal exchange between centre and periphery (SDG 10) and how humanitarian relief serves to keep the Empire and its supply chains intact. Making this explicit can provide opportunities for making humanitarian relief more responsible.

First, recognising politics as necessary for addressing vulnerabilities demands a political reading of the role of LHR. While LHR constructs meaning of humanitarianism as post-political, its histories are defined through politics. LHR has mutual histories and presents with politics of Empire, which is both constituted by and constitutive for the meaning of humanitarianism (Barnett, 2014). However, LHR could equally treat politics as a necessary part of relief action. This could be done, for example, by increasingly asking questions such as what the logistics of abolition looks like or how clandestine humanitarian relief to places like Gaza is organised to subvert surveillance.

Second, the *practices* of delivering humanitarian aid should be scrutinised, starting with the locally desired outcomes. A militarised and securitised LHR focuses on securing the supply rather than serving the needs of humans. A more responsible practice of humanitarianism would not hierarchically convert calculated needs to commodities but would strive to emancipate and understand the visions and needs of affected populations.

Third, responsible organising of humanitarian relief would be organised around responsibility towards crisis-affected people, rather than around accountability towards donors. That way, humanitarian relief would not shape the lives of crisis-affected people to fit a calculation or a neat separation between relief and development but contribute to building grounded sustainable communities (SDG 11). The challenges associated with the three points have been recognised by the humanitarian sector, and many initiatives have been put forth. However, the current form of LHR, dominated by large actors and global supply chains, is unlikely to meaningfully deliver needed responsible transformation to challenge the unequal relations between centre and periphery.

References

Attewell, W. (2018). From factory to field: USAID and the logistics of foreign aid in Soviet-occupied Afghanistan. *Environment and Planning D*, 36(4), 719–738. https://doi.org/10.1177/0263775817711182

Barnett, M. (2014). Refugees and humanitarianism. In Fiddian-Qasmiyeh et al. (eds.) *The Oxford handbook of refugee and forced migration studies*, OUP, 241–252.

Cowen, D. (2014). *The deadly life of logistics: Mapping violence in global trade*, University of Minnesota Press.

Fassin, D. (2007) Humanitarianism as a politics of life. *Public Culture*, 19(3), 499–520. https://doi.org/10.1215/08992363-2007-007

Ferguson, J. (1994). *The anti-politics machine: "Development", depoliticization and bureaucratic power in Lesotho*, University of Minnesota Press.

Hardt, M. & Negri A. (2000) *Empire*, Harvard University Press.

Kovács, G., & Spens, K. M. (2007). Humanitarian logistics in disaster relief operations. *International Journal of Physical Distribution & Logistics Management*, 37(2), 99–114. https://doi.org/10.1108/09600030710734820

Pascucci, E. (2021). More logistics, less aid: Humanitarian-business partnerships and sustainability in the refugee camp. *World Development*, 142, 105424. https://doi.org/10.1016/j.worlddev.2021.105424

Schuller, M. (2016). *Humanitarian aftershocks in Haiti*, Rutgers.

Skinner, R., & Lester, A. (2012). Humanitarianism and empire: New research agendas. *The Journal of Imperial and Commonwealth History*, 40(5), 729–747. https://doi.org/10.1080/03086534.2012.730828

Suwandi, I. (2019). *Value chains: The new economic imperialism*, Monthly Review Press.

Swyngedouw, E. (2011). Interrogating post-democratization: Reclaiming egalitarian political spaces. *Political Geography*, 30(7), 370–380. https://doi.org/10.1016/j.polgeo.2011.08.001

Vannier, C. (2010). Audit culture and grassroots participation in rural Haitian development. *PoLAR*, 33(2), 282–305. https://doi.org/10.1111/j.1555-2934.2010.01115.x

Ziadah, R. (2019). Circulating power: Humanitarian logistics, militarism, and the United Arab Emirates. *Antipode*, 51(5), 1684–1702. https://doi.org/10.1111/anti.12547

Žižek, S. (2006). The lesson of Rancière. In Rancière, J. (ed.) *The politics of aesthetics*, Continuum, 69–79

13 "Corporate saviourism" and poverty in the Global South

Eva Nilsson, Yewondwossen Tesfaye, and Linda Annala Tesfaye

Introduction

This chapter deploys the term "corporate saviourism" to describe multi-stakeholder partnerships in which businesses are engaged in the intentional practice of development in the Global South. The United Nations Sustainable Development Goal (SDG) 17 proposes that a key to transformative action towards sustainable outcomes is to create multi-stakeholder partnerships between governments, non-governmental organisations (NGOs), and businesses. These partnerships are needed to tackle the underlying causes of unsustainability that are systemically interconnected, but they must also be critically scrutinised.

The idea of multi-stakeholder partnerships as a solution to development problems emerged within the UN in the 1990s (Reed & Reed, 2009). At the time, the role of companies in generating development for countries in the Global South went through a radical reformulation. The fall of the Soviet Union and the subsequent ideological victory of neoliberal capitalism (see Chapter 6 for a further discussion), combined with increased criticism by civil society against irresponsible corporate behaviour in different parts of the world, were central factors behind the rise of voluntary Corporate Social Responsibility (CSR) initiatives and multi-stakeholder partnerships between companies, NGOs, and governments. Previously, following decolonisation in the 1960s and until the 1990s, commercial enterprises were promoted by governments in Europe and the USA as "tools" in immanent capitalist "development," meaning providers of jobs, products, and services in the Global South. In the new era since the early 2000s, companies gradually transformed from tools to actors in the intentional practice of development, meaning they became involved in actual development projects (Blowfield & Dolan, 2014 p. 24).

DOI: 10.4324/9781003229728-16

We propose the term corporate saviourism to describe this current era, where corporate-led development interventions are common. We critically examine how these partnerships reproduce a relation of dependence between the "helpers" and the "poor" while simultaneously aiming to transform beneficiaries to self-governed entrepreneurs and consumers connected to global capitalism. We use examples from rural Ethiopia and Tanzania to illustrate our argument. We end with proposing ideas as to how multi-stakeholder partnerships could be reorganised to be more transformative in the quest to end global poverty (SDG 1) and reduce inequalities among countries (SDG 10).

The characteristics of corporate saviourism

With the word "saviourism" we refer to a pattern of behaviour according to which some actors are saviours and others are in need to be saved by them. Similarly to ideologically underpinned "isms" such as racism or sexism that express a belief in the superiority of a certain group over others, saviourism entails a belief in the superiority of the saviours. Saviourism has been used with reference to current practices of development, describing well-meaning acts of "helping" people considered inferior in the Global South while validating existing forms of privilege (Cole, 2012). With the term corporate saviourism, we focus on the central characteristics of the private sector's quest to save people from poverty in the Global South.

During the current era of corporate saviourism, diverse multi-stakeholder partnerships have emerged with the aim of financing, producing knowledge about, and implementing corporate-driven development projects. Public-private finance for development has rocketed as a result of wealthy investors' engagement in philanthropy (McGoey, 2014) and the use of aid resources in financial markets (Järvelä & Solitander, 2020).

The knowledge production for corporate-led development has been generated jointly by companies, NGOs, trade unions, consumers, CSR consultants, and shareholders. To generate the discursive power (Foucault, 1972) of corporate-led development, these actors commonly come together in roundtables and events in the Global North to discuss and develop new international standards and to present case studies from their engagements with local communities in the Global South. An emotional experience of "doing good" is stimulated when companies that perform best against different CSR indexes and standards are awarded (Rajak, 2011).

On national and local levels in the Global South, companies form coalitions with NGOs, community-based organisations, and consultants to finance and implement development projects (Rajak, 2011, Reed & Reed, 2009). In these partnerships, poverty has generally been problematised as a product of market failure and interventions have been driven by a conviction that markets can work for the poor. In practice, corporate-led development interventions have provided benefi-ciaries with basic capabilities for economic participation by supporting skills in entrepreneurship and professions that investors lack labour for, such as engineering, welding or catering. They have also introduced new products for people at the bottom of the economic "pyramid" to con-sume (cf. Prahalad, 2006).

What these partnerships have in common is a neoliberal governance rationale, a governmentality that aims to install the ideas of entrepre-neurship and individualised responsibility into society and to create human capital for a capitalist social order while depoliticising questions related to inequitable distribution of wealth, entitlement, and rights (Blowfield & Dolan, 2014; Shamir, 2008). Governmentality refers here to the practices of power used to govern people's conduct (Foucault, 1991). In partnerships, neoliberal governmentality is enacted through interventions among people that seemingly lack the capacity to respon-sibly conduct themselves. Within the "lack of capacity" narrative, the idea of corporate saviourism emerges as a powerful governing tool to "help the poor" through market-led development solutions. These practices of corporate saviourism confound two very different logics; that of development cooperation where structures of dependency and reciprocity are built and that of a depersonalised market economy with unrestricted competition (Rajak, 2011).

Corporate saviourism in rural Ethiopia and Tanzania

In two different examples that we have researched in rural Ethiopia and Tanzania, private and public actors have formed partnerships for finan-cing, knowledge production, and implementation of projects that tackle poverty-related problems. These partnerships exemplify corporate saviourism in action.

In our first example, the NGO Oxfam America, operating in the Amhara region in Ethiopia, has implemented a project that provides wea-ther insurance for farmers against rising drought risk. During the time of data collection in 2016, the project was implemented in Northern parts of Ethiopia and had been financed and advised by one of the world's largest insurance companies Swiss Re and the philanthropic financier Rockefeller Foundation. A local insurance company (Nyala Insurance) in association with governmental and non-governmental micro-finance institutions and community development actors implemented the project. The International Research Institute for Climate and Society at Columbia University in New York City has provided technical support in terms of reading and compiling satellite data. These actors announced their joint commitment at a Clinton Global Initiative (CGI) meeting in New York in 2009. The CGI is an organisation set up by former US President Bill Clinton that brings "leaders" from across sectors to drive action to address global challenges. Actors in the Global North have dominated the initial financial partnership and the knowledge production within it.

In our second example, some of the world's largest fossil fuel companies, Shell and Equinor, have implemented several projects in the Lindi and Mtwara regions in Tanzania after making significant gas discoveries in the area in 2012–2015. In making voluntary "sustainability investments," the companies have partnered with international and local NGOs and government institutions. The two companies, together with governments from countries such as Norway, Germany, and the UK have mainly acted in the role of financiers, while development consultancies such as German GIZ and NGOs like the UK-based charity Voluntary Service Overseas have been involved in the implementation of the projects. The most common aim in Shell and Equinor's development interventions has been to promote entrepreneurship and self-employment for young Tanzanians. One example of this is the "Farming is Business" project managed by GIZ and implemented by the Aga Khan Foundation, an international faith-based NGO. The project supported local farmers, entrepreneurs, and small businesses in the Mtwara and Lindi regions by linking them to markets and catering opportunities in the extractive industry and adjacent sectors. It also supported farmers' production, organisational, and business skills.

The actors in both examples have been united around the idea that markets can solve poverty-related problems. In the example from Ethiopia, poverty has been tackled through a "bottom-of-the pyramid" approach, turning farmers into consumers in the global risk insurance market in exchange for self-employment. In the Tanzanian example actors have shared the objective to tackle poverty through inclusion into the value chains of the global gas economy. The companies' interventions have been motivated by the business case argument, meaning that they are considered to benefit business in the long term.

A central component of both projects has been to "change mindsets" from dependants to responsible, self-governed individuals, in other words, to transform the beneficiaries into neoliberal subjects. Despite this intention to "empower" beneficiaries to be responsible and self-governed (Ilcan & Lacey, 2011), in both cases, they have been represented as dependent subjects that need intervention undertaken by corporate saviours to become rational subjects. For example, in Ethiopia, the insurance package has been presented as a life changing solution and the insurer as the dominant development actor. Constructing farmers through the realm of development or as dependent subjects requiring help, the bargaining power of farmers to make free choices over different insurance products has been suffocated.

The realities of both examples are complex and contradictory, and we are only able to give a tiny glimpse of them here. The projects are met as much with hope as with reluctance and contestation. From a macro perspective it can be argued, however, that in both examples the root causes of inequality are left untouched. Further, the manner in which these projects are implemented through technical implementation, monitoring and evaluation frameworks, does not only exclude root causes, but it also depoliticises them (Li, 2007). Access to and control over the value chains and technologies involved in the projects remain in the hands of the corporate saviours and the unequal distribution of power and wealth persists. On a micro-level, life-worlds of the beneficiaries are ruptured by discourses and practices of commodification, capital accumulation, and profit making. A neoliberal epistemology, where market-based social relations have penetrated lives (Shamir, 2008, p. 3), has been donated to people in an act of goodwill.

Conclusion

In resonance with SDG 17 on building effective partnerships for sustainable development, we argue that poverty reduction (SDG 1) requires various types of knowledges and actors. However, we remain critical of the transformative potential of multi-stakeholder partnerships with corporations, such as the ones described in our empirical cases. In these partnerships, the solution to poverty is expanding global capitalism to spaces where it is yet to gain ground rather than creating alternative structures which foster more equitable social relations and increase people's economic, political, and social power.

These market-based and technical solutions to systemic problems not only exclude root causes for poverty, but they also tend to depoliticise them. Expressions of dissent that would be required to challenge the solutions mobilised by powerful actors are often illegitimated in the presence of a hegemonic market logic (Fougère & Solitander, 2020). Although NGOs are present as non-market actors in both multi-stakeholder partnerships described in this chapter, the voices and interests of the local people may not be represented through them, contrary to what is commonly assumed (Banerjee, 2014).

For partnerships to be transformative, the acknowledgement and dismantling of power inequalities between the various actors is crucial (SDG 10). Although we recognise the boundaries and limitations of corporate actors in realising a systemic change in the global capitalist order, we call for a serious reflection by corporate actors and their partners on their anticipated role as saviours of the poor. In addition to imposing supposedly empowering neoliberal epistemologies on the "bottom billion" (Roy, 2012), we point to the concurrent dependency-generating practice and victimising discourse of "helping the poor" that is common in interventions in the Global South. For partnerships to be more transformative, people and inclusive governments from the Global South should be the main power holders in them. They should not be rendered dependent on corporate goodwill or victimised through hierarchical discourses.

Acknowledgements

This work has been supported by the Finnish Cultural Foundation (grant number: 00210775) and the Foundation for Economic Education in Finland (grant number: 200046).

References

Banerjee, S. B. (2014). A critical perspective on corporate social responsibility: Towards a global governance framework. *Critical Perspectives on International Business*, 10(1–2), 84–95. https://doi.org/10.1108/cpoib-06-2013-0021

Blowfield, M. & Dolan, C. (2014). Business as a development agent: Evidence of possibility and improbability. *Third World Quarterly*, 35(1), 22–42. https://doi.org/ 10.1080/01436597.2013.868982

Cole, T. (2012). 'The White-Savior Industrial Complex'. *The Atlantic* 21.3.2012. Retrieved 28 September 2021 from www.theatlantic.com/international/archive/2012/03/the-white-savior-industrial-complex/254843/

Foucault, M. (1972). *The archaeology of knowledge*. New York, NY: Pantheon.

Foucault, M. (1991). Governmentality. In Burchell, G., Gordon, C. and Miller, P., (eds.). *The Foucault effect: Studies in governmentality*, pp. 87–104. Chicago, IL: University of Chicago Press.

Fougère, M. & Solitander, N. (2020). Dissent in Consensusland: An agonistic problematization of multistakeholder governance. *Journal of Business Ethics*, 164, 683–699. https://doi.org/ 10.1007/s10551-019-04398-z

Ilcan, S. & Lacey, A. (2011). *Governing the poor: Exercises of poverty reduction, practices of global aid*. Montreal: McGill-Queen's University Press.

92   *Eva Nilsson, Yewondwossen Tesfaye, and Linda Annala Tesfaye*

Järvelä, J. & Solitander, N. (2020). The financialization and responsibilization of development aid. In Lund-Thomsen, P., Wendelboe Hansen, M. & Lindgreen, A. (eds.). *Business and development studies: Issues and perspectives*, pp. 235–256. London: Routledge. https://doi.org/10.4324/9781315163338

Li, T. (2007). *The will to improve: Governmentality, development, and the practice of politics*. Durham: Duke University Press.

McGoey, L. (2014). The philanthropic state: Market-state hybrids in the philanthrocapitalist turn. *Third World Quarterly*, 35(1), 109–125. https://doi.org/10.1080/01436597.2014.868989

Prahalad, C. K. (2006). *The fortune at the bottom of the pyramid*. Upper Saddle River, NJ: Wharton School Pub.

Rajak, D. (2011). *In good company: An anatomy of corporate social responsibility*. Stanford, CA: Stanford University Press.

Reed, A. M., & Reed, D. (2009). Partnerships for development: Four models of business involvement. *Journal of Business Ethics*, 90(Suppl. 1), 3–37. https://doi.org/10.1007/s10551-008-9913-y

Roy, A. (2012). Ethical subjects: Market rule in an age of poverty. *Public Culture*, 24(1), 105–108. https://doi.org/10.1215/08992363-1443574

Shamir, R. (2008). The age of responsibilization: On market-embedded morality. *Economy and Society*, 37(1), 1–19. https://doi.org/10.1080/03085140701760833

14 Social media and bias 2.0

Anna Maaranen, Frank den Hond, and Mikko Vesa

Introduction

This chapter discusses algorithmic bias – or what we call bias 2.0 – on social media. It argues that while new technologies utilising advanced algorithms that are often referred to as artificial intelligence have inspired hopes of a world beyond bias, the reality is gloomier. On today's social media, interaction, access, and visibility are largely orchestrated by algorithms that are not free from bias but, instead, have learnt to efficiently automate it.

With the emergence of the Internet and the World Wide Web in the 1990s, hopes were high for this new "information superhighway" to democratise societies by providing a more equal access to information, markets, and education. At the heart of this optimism was an essentially modernist development narrative. Social media was to give better access to the classical devices of progress and enlightenment, which by default would solve a multitude of human and societal problems. Some decades later, many observers are increasingly concerned that the digital revolution is turning on its head and becoming a source of problems, in addition to solving them.

On the one hand, there is techno-optimist talk of the fourth industrial revolution or the second machine age in the domain of industrial production (Brynjolfsson & McAfee, 2014). On the other hand, the web itself is construed as becoming a new iron cage of capitalist control (Zuboff, 2019). It turns out that the information superhighway of high hopes has become the domain of big tech, whose business models use social media, "Web 2.0," for the accumulation and analysis of massively big data. An increasing concern here is algorithmic bias which has implications for responsible organising in that it can reinforce inequalities in society in a newly difficult-to-track way.

DOI: 10.4324/9781003229728-17

Bias is bad as it fosters incorrect conclusions and misunderstandings about the phenomenon of interest, or about the world as it exists. Such bias may result from multiple sources such as (1) reliance on incomplete, partial, or otherwise untrustworthy information as if it were reliable data, (2) the digitalisation of information, and (3) the treatment of accidental, spurious correlations and patterns in data as meaningful. Hence, bias needs to be avoided, and if technology can help reduce or even eliminate bias, then that technology is valuable for that precise reason. A case in point is social media: when the technology was introduced, back in the 1990s, Web 2.0 sparked the idea of a globally accessible digital space where users could interact and create as well as consume content free from editorial control and other filters that mediate information provision. Social media were thus perceived as inherently participatory spaces driven by increased informality, continuous uploads, and user-generated content.

On social media, nearly everyone with access to the Internet can create, consume, and engage with content independent of their geographical location, social status, or financial situation. A notable example is the facilitation of social movement activism. Social media were thus not only expected to allow more people to participate in information exchange but also to reduce bias in information exchanges, and for these two reasons, to enhance democracy. However, this has proved to be more complicated and problematic than anticipated.

What has only recently become visible is how, and how consequentially, social media are being orchestrated by the algorithms on which they operate. Each social media platform has its own algorithms, but their common function is to determine access to and visibility of content on a given platform through collection, processing, and presentation of user data. On today's social media, interaction is orchestrated by this decision-making technology running in the background. Social media algorithms predict users' future interests through pattern matching of stored historical data on clicks, searches, likes, and other personal and biographical data, and they determine what kind of content a given user is shown and what remains hidden from their view. For example, Facebook's timeline, the results from a Google search, and the recommendations on Netflix are all carefully curated, based not just on your previously espoused preferences but also on those by numerous others.

Algorithms and curation are not without consequences. By customising users' online encounters with content and other users, social media enhance the tendency of people to be attracted to and brought together with content they are likely to enjoy and people who are "similar" to them. This phenomenon is known as homophily (McPherson et al., 2001). Exploiting people's curiosity and their tendency to pay more attention to "spectacular" than to neutral information, algorithms have become effective in connecting similar people and trapping them in echo chambers and filter bubbles. Algorithms raise barriers to accessing in online spaces content that is outside of one's historical trajectory, to encountering people dissimilar to oneself, and to learning about views alternative to one's own. Instead of eliminating bias, we argue, a "bias 2.0" is now in place.

Manufacturing bias 2.0

How did this bias 2.0 come into being? Algorithms are fed with or collect themselves numerous data inputs from social media users and then construct user profiles; some of the attributes in user profiles (e.g., gender, sexual orientation, and political views) are inferred through a pattern matching calculus on the data of numerous users. Bias 2.0 can emerge at two moments. It may emerge, first, during the collection of historical records of user data, due to reliance on the assumption that user data elucidate something meaningful about the user, that an accurate picture can be created from likes, clicks, and other traces and trails that a user leaves when wandering around in the virtual space of social media.

Second, bias 2.0 may emerge from the processing of data in pattern matching calculus, including the "learning" about associations in massive data sets. This relies on the assumption that similarities in user data reflect similarities in users, that we can rely on the procedural rationality and calculus of which Simon (1996) speaks so highly, but which leave little or no space for other, substantive kinds of rationalities (cf. Lindebaum et al., 2020; Moser et al., 2021). Neither assumption is fault proof.

Consequently, there are numerous reports of, for example, algorithmic discrimination due to (mis)attribution of gender (Fosch-Villaronga et al., 2021). Racist algorithmic outcomes have also received increasing attention, for example, when facial recognition systems did not perform well on dark skin tones (Klare et al., 2012) or when shown faces of women and transgender people (Scheuerman et al., 2020). Arguably, pictures exhibiting men's faces were overrepresented in the training set for facial recognition.

It is thus evident that visibility and access in social media spaces is prone to many of the same inequalities that the promise of the Web 2.0 was meant to tackle. Designed with hopes of cherishing diversity and equality, social media have instead become a space of technologically administered homophily, where social injustice, exclusion, and discrimination remain (Fosch-Villaronga et al., 2021). Algorithmic decision-making re-enacts whatever biases already existed "irl" (in real life) and occasionally even introduces new ones, for example when it acts on spurious associations.

While social media are not the only technology to use algorithmic decision-making, they are a case in point of online spaces where algorithmic bias has widespread impact. Algorithms are a novel set of non-human social actors, numerous and obscure, that work their way around the online sphere (Gruwell, 2018). Yet, who is to be held accountable for the biases they create and disseminate? They embody the biases of those who develop and use them and create new biases through their processing of user data. However, it is often impossible to know whether and how they are biased and where their biases come from. What once was human bias has become an automated bias 2.0: human bias has been translated into and reshaped by algorithms that replicate and reinforce it in the vastness of the global social media space.

This has prompted calls for increased algorithmic transparency and regulation in online spaces. However, many of these discussions tend to treat algorithmic fairness as a primarily technical issue of data processing (Wong, 2020). What these studies do not address are the deeper-rooted ethical and responsibility-related concerns related to algorithmic bias. If algorithmic processes are essentially chained moments of choice in which a variety of human and non-human actors are engaged (Rieder, 2017), who are to be held responsible for those moments: algorithms, their designers and programmers, the social media companies commercialising them, or the platform users who interact with them? And who makes the call on whether they are "fair"? How do agency, morality, and responsibility interrelate in the online space where encounters between people and technology increasingly blur? Responding to such questions requires tackling the complex notion of ethics and morality in an age where algorithmic technology has become a key element of our social – or rather, socio-techno-logical – structure.

Conclusion

In this chapter, we have discussed how social media algorithms reinforce biases related to, for example, gender and race. Our discussion sparks concerns related to the United Nations Sustainable Development Goals (SDGs). There is ample evidence on algorithmic discrimination, sexism, and racism indicating that, through what we call "bias 2.0," social media works against achieving gender equality (SDG 5) and reducing inequalities (SDG 10). Work to mitigate or counter algorithmic bias on social media can make progress on these SDGs and reduce inequalities in online spaces.

Moreover, bias 2.0 in social media links to another goal: promoting equal education and lifelong learning opportunities for all (SDG 4). In 2021, more than half of the world's population uses social media, and the number is quickly growing. Social media platforms become increasingly prominent in our daily lives, and information and knowledge are increasingly spread through social media. Their prominence makes digital media literacy a major concern. Promoting not only equal access to but also comprehension and literacy of online spaces and their socio-technological features such as algorithms is essential for reducing barriers to knowledge, learning, and societal participation and enabling lifelong learning opportunities for all. However, only by addressing bias 2.0 can social media and other online spaces fulfil the promise of democratising knowledge.

References

Brynjolfsson, E., & McAfee, A. (2014). *The Second Machine Age*. New York, NY: W W Norton.

Fosch-Villaronga, E., Poulsen, A., Søraa, R. A., & Custers, B. H. M. (2021). A little bird told me your gender: Gender inferences in social media. *Information Processing & Management*, *58*(3), 102541. https://doi.org/10.1016/j.ipm.2021.102541.

Gruwell, L. (2018). Constructing research, constructing the platform: Algorithms and the rhetoricity of social media research. *Present Tense*, *6*(3). Available from www.presenttensejournal.org/wp-content/uploads/2018/06/Gruwell.pdf.

Klare, B. F., Burge, M. J., Klontz, J. C., Bruegge, R. W. V., & Jain, A. K. (2012). Face recognition performance: Role of demographic information. *IEEE Transactions on Information Forensics and Security*, *7*(6), 1789–1801. https://doi.org/10.1109/TIFS.2012.2214212.

Lindebaum, D., Vesa, M., & den Hond, F. (2020). Insights from *The Machine Stops* to better understand rational assumptions in algorithmic decision-making and its implications for organizations. *Academy of Management Review*, *45*(1), 247–263. https://doi.org/10.5465/amr.2018.0181.

McPherson, M., Smith-Lovin, L., & Cook, J. M. (2001). Birds of a feather: Homophily in social networks. *Annual Review of Sociology*, *27*(1), 415–444. https://doi.org/10.1146/annurev.soc.27.1.415.

Moser, C., den Hond, F., & Lindebaum, D. (2021). Morality in the age of artificially intelligent algorithms. *Academy of Management Learning & Education*. https://doi.org/10.5465/amle.2020.0287.

98 *Anna Maaranen, Frank den Hond, and Mikko Vesa*

Rieder, B. (2017). Scrutinizing an algorithmic technique: The Bayes classifier as interested reading of reality. *Information, Communication & Society, 20*(1), 100–117. https://doi.org/10.1080/1369118X.2016.1181195.

Scheuerman, M. K., Wade, K., Lustig, C., & Brubaker, J. R. (2020). How we've taught algorithms to see identity: Constructing race and gender in image databases for facial analysis. *Proceedings of the ACM on Human-Computer Interaction, 4*(CSCW1), 1–35. https://doi.org/10.1145/3392866.

Simon, H. A. (1996). *The Sciences of the Artificial* (3rd Ed.). Cambridge, MA: MIT Press.

Wong, P. H. (2020). Democratizing algorithmic fairness. *Philosophy & Technology, 33*(2), 225–244. https://doi.org/10.1007/s13347-019-00355-w.

Zuboff, S. (2019). *The Age of Surveillance Capitalism.* New York, NY: PublicAffairs.

15 Intersectional inequalities and how to fight them

Inkeri Tanhua and Neema Komba

Introduction

This chapter discusses how different systems of social inequality – such as those related to gender, marital status, and social class – intersect and create intersectional inequalities experienced by groups and individuals. As an example, we discuss inequalities experienced by women working on their husbands' coffee farms in Tanzania. Understanding how and why unequal systems have emerged helps in fighting them. We argue that equality needs to be promoted at the local level, in organising families and societies, as well as at the structural level, including in legislation and frameworks such as the United Nations Sustainable Development Goals (SDGs). This chapter addresses several SDGs in the context of responsible coffee production (SDG 12): in addition to promoting gender equality (SDG 5) and reducing inequalities (SDG 10), we address quality education (SDG 4) and decent work (SDG 8).

The strengths of intersectional analyses lie in the simultaneous focus on multiple social categorisations and related inequalities, and the emphasis on the role of power relations in causing social inequalities (Collins & Bilge, 2016, pp. 1–13). By recognising power relations that are causing inequalities, our chapter addresses some of the shortcomings of the concept of diversity discussed in Chapter 3. In addition, our discussion highlights the necessity to explore contexts in the Global South on their own terms, openly discussing the social categorisations that need to be considered in intersectional analysis.

Intersectionality as an analytical lens

The concept of intersectionality is an attempt to refocus diversity research and practical equality and diversity work. Many critical researchers (Castro & Holvino, 2016; Collins & Bilge, 2016; Lykke, 2010)

DOI: 10.4324/9781003229728-18

and practitioners alike use the term intersectionality instead of, or in addition to, diversity. We draw on a Nordic scholar, Nina Lykke (2010), who defines intersectionality as a tool to analyse how historically specific kinds of power differentials and constraining normativities – based on categorisations such as gender, ethnicity, race, class, sexuality, age, and dis/ability – interact and produce societal inequalities and unjust social relations.

In comparison to the concept of diversity, the strengths of intersectionality are that it reminds us of power relations as a cause of social inequalities and of the need to focus on multiple social categorisations at the same time. It is not enough that one focuses on diversity of people; one also has to consider how these diversities are used in constituting a myriad of inequalities. With its roots in the inequalities experienced by black women in the USA (Collins, 2000; Crenshaw, 1991), intersectionality also emphasises the need to discuss racism and colonialism.

However, there are some precautions that need to be considered before applying intersectional analysis in African contexts. Although intersectional analyses have been used by many authors globally, including many authors in the Global South, most research that uses the term intersectionality is American- and European-focused. African contexts need to be explored on their own terms; the range of meaningful social categorisations may be considerably different to the earlier literature (Meer & Müller, 2017). For example, we consider the category of marital status, which is explored less in American and European intersectional research but very meaningful in our Tanzanian example. The specific history of Tanzania must be considered in investigating how the current power differentials and inequalities have emerged.

Often, intersectional inequalities have emerged when practices, structures, and legislation are designed for those who fit into the prevalent norms that usually reflect dominant groups in the society at the current time. For instance, colonial times and norms during those times have influenced the current (irresponsible) organisation of coffee production in Tanzania. Although gendered divisions of labour were not invented only by colonial powers, the colonial state – as well as the post-colonial state today – were complicit in efforts to sustain patriarchal structures of power, which underpin the local peasant economy (Mbilinyi, 2016). The current way of irresponsible organising benefits not only the former colonial powers that enjoy coffee products in the Global North, but also certain (although not all) local groups of men in the coffee industry in Tanzania.

Intersectional inequalities in Tanzania

> I used to sell my coffee through a colleague for many years. One day I gave her about ten kilograms. She never gave me the payment. I couldn't complain since it was a stolen coffee from my husband.
>
> (Participant in coffee theft network,
> as cited in Komba, 2021)

We draw on the socio-economic histography of coffee production in the Mbinga district in Tanzania, written by Yustina Komba (2021), and discuss why married women are still today excluded from reaping the benefit of their labour in coffee production. Coffee has historically been a male dominated product, with women being side-lined from collecting income despite their labour being crucial in coffee production (Fowler-Salamini, 2002; Komba, 2021). Due to their exclusion, women may end up selling coffee unofficially without telling their husbands, as described in the extract above.

Coffee is a significant export product for Tanzania, generating five per cent of its total export earnings and contributing about three per cent of Tanzanian GDP. As smallholder farms produce nearly 90 per cent of the coffee, it provides a direct income to approximately 400,000 households. It is a crucial income for many families and helps in achieving various SDGs (Pyk & Hatab, 2018). For instance, coffee is an important source of income for farmers to pay their children's school fees (Anderson et al., 2016).

However, all people involved in growing coffee do not benefit equally. As shown in the histography of coffee production in the Mbinga district (Komba, 2021), women hold a weak position in coffee production due to patriarchal land tenure systems and farming practices. When coffee production was introduced during the colonial era, only men were given coffee seeds to plant, as they were considered permanent residents on the land while women were considered temporary residents because they would get married and relocate. Due to patrilineal inheritance, married women owned neither their fathers' nor husbands' land (Komba, 2021). Reforms to the Tanzanian land act were made in 1999 to ensure a more equitable distribution of land, but the reforms did not touch the general statutory recognition of customary laws that govern women's inheritance of land (Dancer, 2017).

Despite their inability to own land and coffee farms, women have always worked on their fathers' or husbands' farms, doing nearly everything alongside them. During the colonial era, there were only a few tasks, which women were not considered suitable for. These tasks included pest control and pruning, which were considered more "professional" and hence masculine, and required training that only men could receive during that time (Komba, 2021, p. 237). The inequal distribution of agricultural education further contributed to the exclusion of women in key areas of coffee production and decision-making. Both women and men were, however, irrigating seedlings, planting them, weeding, mulching, using fertilisers, harvesting coffee, pulping, drying, sorting, and delivering coffee to the market centres, and selling it. Despite this, women were not allowed to collect the payments by themselves – a legacy that continues today.

The intersection of gender, marital status, and social class creates exploitation of women in coffee production. Although today women can legally own land, many women working in their husbands' coffee farms do not have the resources to purchase land, which their brothers or husbands often have inherited. By rendering them unable to own land, the women are also excluded from co-operative unions that are the primary means for coffee selling and marketing decisions.

Since coffee is a cash crop for export, coffee farmers are a bit better off compared to some other groups of smallholder farmers. However, most of them are still rather poor; most coffee farmers rely on family labour to produce coffee and own less than five acres of land (Ruben et al., 2018). Many coffee producers lack social safety nets and are vulnerable to global price fluctuations, increasing input prices, and climate change. As an example, when faced with medical bills or school fees, many smallholder coffee farmers are forced to sell their produce at unprofitable prices. Smallholder farmers produce 95 per cent of the coffee in Tanzania but only gain 41 per cent of the value, the rest going to other players in the value chain (Ruben et al., 2018). These economic and social conditions, together with patriarchal systems, contribute to keeping married women in smallholder farming as unpaid labour on their husbands' farms, without having a voice in coffee production.

Recently, the number of women in cooperatives in Mbinga have increased to meet the requirements of certifications such as Fairtrade and Rainforest Alliance (Komba, 2021). However, reforming existing inequalities requires a combination of efforts. In the case of Tanzanian agricultural labour, repealing discriminatory customary laws of inheritance, combined with education and societal engagement in these reforms would improve the position of women in land tenure practices (Dancer, 2017). In addition, increasing women's educational level would improve women's share in land ownership and increase agricultural labour returns (Palacios-Lopez et al., 2017). Agricultural training of both women and men is also important and improves the adoption of sustainable agricultural practices and increases agricultural returns (Pyk & Hatab, 2018). Furthermore, initiatives that promote equality and equity at family level such as Kahawa ya Kesho, which promotes gender equality and joint decision-making (at family level) among smallholder coffee farmers (Baxter, 2019), are needed to improve women's position in agriculture.

Conclusion

We have used an intersectional approach and historical research to analyse inequalities experienced by married women working for their husbands' coffee farms in Tanzania. Our example highlights that it is crucial to critically examine which are the relevant social categorisations to include in the analysis in each local context. In our Tanzanian example, it was relevant to consider the intersection of gender, marital status, and social class, even though marital status is mostly not mentioned in the American- and European-focused literature. While the coffee example demonstrates the inequalities (SDGs 5, 10) that exist in agricultural labour and income in Tanzania, the core of the problem lies in how society is organised around land ownership, provision of education (SDG 4), division of labour, and family decision-making. Also, specific colonial and post-colonial histories of Tanzania are relevant for understanding how power differentials related to social categorisations have emerged in this context and continue to operate today.

An intersectional approach encourages to examine how various inequality systems impact simultaneously. Although women can legally own land in Tanzania – and some unmarried or widowed women smallholder farmers or women from higher social classes do – owning land is very difficult for married women in smallholder farming because they often lack means to earn income to purchase land. Decent work (SDG 8) for these women would mean that they could profit from their labour and be included in decision-making in the co-operatives.

Acknowledgements

This work was supported by the Foundation for Economic Education in Finland (grant numbers: 190184 and 200289).

References

Anderson, J., Learch, C. E., & Gardner, S. T. (2016). National survey and segmentation of smallholder households in Tanzania: Understanding their demand for financial, agricultural and digital solutions. In *CGAP Working Paper*.

Baxter, W. (2019). Tanzania Coffee Fuels Youth Employment Project. Retrieved 30 September 2021 from www.crs.org/stories/tanzania-coffee-fuels-youth-employment-project

Castro, M. R., & Holvino, E. (2016). Applying intersectionality in organizations: Inequality markers, cultural scripts and advancement practices in a professional service firm. *Gender, Work and Organization, 23*(3), 328–347. https://doi.org/10.1111/gwao.12129

Collins, P. H. (2000). *Black feminist thought: Knowledge, consciousness, and the political empowerment* (2nd ed.). New York and London: Routledge.

Collins, P. H., & Bilge, S. (2016). *Intersectionality*. Cambridge: Polity Press.

Crenshaw, K. (1991). Mapping the margins: Intersectionality, identity politics, and violence against women of color. *Stanford Law Review, 43*(6), 1241–1299.

Dancer, H. (2017). An equal right to inherit? Women's land rights, customary law and constitutional reform in Tanzania. *Social and Legal Studies, 26*(3), 291–310. https://doi.org/10.1177/0964663916677560

Fowler-Salamini, H. (2002). Women coffee sorters confront the mill owners and the Veracruz revolutionary state, 1915-1918. *Journal of Women's History, 14*(1), 34–63. https://doi.org/10.1353/jowh.2002.0027

Komba, Y. S. (2021). *A socio-economic history of coffee production in Mbinga District, Tanzania, c .1920 – 2015*. Stellenbosch: University of Stellenbosch.

Lykke, N. (2010). *Feminist studies: A guide to intersectional theory, methodology and writing*. New York, NY: Routledge.

Mbilinyi, M. (2016). Review of African political economy analysing the history of agrarian struggles in Tanzania from a feminist perspective. *Review of African Political Economy, 43*, 115–129. https://doi.org/10.1080/03056244.2016.1219036

Meer, T., & Müller, A. (2017). Considering intersectionality in Africa. *Agenda. Empowering Women for Gender Equity, 31*(1), 3–4. https://doi.org/10.1080/10130950.2017.1363583

Palacios-Lopez, A., Christiaensen, L., & Kilic, T. (2017). How much of the labor in African agriculture is provided by women? *Food Policy, 67*, 52–63. https://doi.org/10.1016/j.foodpol.2016.09.017

Pyk, F., & Hatab, A. A. (2018). Fairtrade and sustainability: Motivations for Fairtrade certification among smallholder coffee growers in Tanzania. *Sustainability, 10*(1551). https://doi.org/10.3390/su10051551

Ruben, R., Allen, C., Boureima, F., Mhando, D. G., & Dijkxhoorn, Y. (2018). *Coffee value chain analysis in the Southern Highlands of Tanzania*. Report for the European Commission, DG-DEVCO. Value chain analysis for development project (VCA4D CTR 2016/375-804), 135p + annexes. Wageningen: Wageningen University & Research.

16 Work, care, and gendered (in)equalities

Charlotta Niemistö and Jeff Hearn

Introduction

This chapter discusses the (ir)responsible organising of systems of production and reproduction through work and care, highlighting the inequalities – pertaining to gender, but also age, class, and ethnicity – in how work and care are valued and distributed. Questions of work and care closely link to equality and justice more generally, as the intersection of gender, (younger and older) age, class, and ethnicity often contributes to discrimination in and beyond working life. This is at least partly due to gendered assumptions about care being seen as "less" and primarily as something women should do. Such assumptions often do not fit the masculinist image of the "ideal worker" devoted to the work organisation and not having competing responsibilities, such as care responsibilities outside of the work sphere (Acker, 1990). Unequal distribution of work and care lead to severe economic disadvantages for those providing informal unpaid care to others, compared to those who devote themselves to paid work. Responsible organising of work and care, or paid and unpaid work, would see both as equally valuable.

As the social relations of work and care constitute fundamental aspects of gender relations in society, strong and persistently remaining gendered assumptions are embedded in systems of production and reproduction. We examine some key inequalities and interrelations in systems of production and reproduction, in terms of gender, age, life phases, work, and care, drawing on interview data with professionals in management careers in different countries in the Global North. We focus on the importance of temporal and spatial boundaries between work and care, in different ages and life phases (Hearn et al., 2021). We contribute to discussions on gender equality (United Nations Sustainable Development Goal, SDG 5), but also to broader discussions on well-being (SDG 3), decent work (SDG 8), and inequalities (SDG 10).

DOI: 10.4324/9781003229728-19

Gender, age, and the uneven distribution of work and care

In many contemporary careers, individual autonomy and flexibility in the work is high, yet flexibility can – especially in current post-industrial knowledge organisations – be treated synonymously with availability outside of office hours and blurring boundaries between paid work and non-work time, which can lead to boundarylessness for workers in post-industrial work in the Global North (Field & Chan, 2018). Simultaneously, "long hours" working culture remains strong and often unchallenged in many sectors. This creates extensive pressure in balancing, managing, and coping with work and care responsibilities. Additionally, the expectations of the "ideal worker" are increasingly applying to men, women, and further genders alike.

Work and care are themselves unevenly gendered, often very much so, and unequally distributed in different life phases. Women, most often seen as and being primary caretakers, may carry a "double" or "triple burden," not only required to be the "ideal worker" but separately or simultaneously caring for different dependents, such as children, parents, friends, neighbours, partners, and grandchildren. Such gendered care includes caring about, taking care of, giving care, receiving care, and caring with (Tronto, 1993, 2013).

These gendered realities and constraints are often played down in organisations and in societies, and in how working life is organised (Lewis et al., 2007). However, the responsible organising of production and reproduction (work and care) is key for social sustainability (Littig & Griessler, 2005): "no production system operates without a reproduction system … its intimate Other" (Troung, 1996, p. 47). The intertwining of work and care affects how work is organised and everyday experiences of individuals in work organisations and elsewhere. Furthermore, this intertwining links to the structured existence, yet often ambiguity, of boundaries between private and public realms, between work and care, and across spatial and temporal boundaries in working life and organisations (as recognised in feminist and postcolonial perspectives; Hearn & Hobson, 2020; Tronto, 1993, 2013). While care and caring typically occur in interpersonal proximity, they are more generally to be understood within the global political economy of care, as, for example, with care chains, whereby different people, marked as visible by their subordination, and mainly women, give care to others, typically more privileged.

Intersections of gender, age, work, and care are significant in how different understandings of shifting life situations and phases are constructed in gendered, aged, classed, and ethnicised/racialised terms, not fully recognised in the organisation of working life. Recognising the importance of social sustainability challenges, such as the need to reduce inequalities, urges us to see work and care as intertwined rather than as separate domains, where one or the other, often meaning care, can be downplayed or even ignored in work organisations.

Experiences of blurring boundaries between work and care

The strongly blurring boundaries in knowledge work, where time, place, and non-work identity can easily lose meaning, create new everyday patterns. Attending to care responsibilities for a few hours every day in late afternoon and early evening may mean attending to work tasks remotely in the late evenings and during weekends. In our data, from interviews with global professionals in high-pressure knowledge work in the Global North, this was the pattern from middle management upwards, leading to boundaries between work and home often becoming permeable. At the same time, they had to accommodate to the "ideal worker" model. The women in particular struggled with this, while many of the men managers had partners who carried the majority of care responsibilities. In many cases, work took up most of the waking time and emotional energy of the women, and work was at the top of personal priorities even when not working:

> I really don't stop thinking of work, I do my bed and I wake up and I think about it. That's something I need to fix, for me. I think it's just me though 'cause I have a lot on, I'm very busy [...] I'd say most of us are probably like that. I'd say some people have an ability to switch of better than others. I switch off on Saturday and Sunday. But Monday to Friday I don't switch off [...] I try very hard to keep Saturday and Sunday for my children, I'm a mom, and [on weekdays] those two hours half past six to half eight I'm a mom and otherwise I'm at work.
>
> (Female middle manager in a B2B company,
> 40s, two children, Ireland)

The same respondent makes use of her commuting time to keep up social relationships and care of an elderly parent:

> I have another friend who has the same life as me, and we're both in the same traffic jam, every day, we call each other nearly every day on the way home, and I call my mom on the way home.

The difficulty in organising knowledge-intensive work can reproduce gendered structures around organising work and care, as women are typically responsible for the majority of care given (Pfau-Effinger, 2005). Organising work and career to enable care starts for women already before having care responsibilities; many women feel pressured between career and motherhood expectations when starting to plan a family (Niemistö et al., 2021a, b). Not having time, or the right time, to have a child was also reported in our data. This was present as a sad reflection that there never was time from work to find someone to start a family with or how having children was not a straightforward process, even if the circumstances around it would be well planned. Some of the women spoke of postponing childbearing for many years, wanting to ensure a more "secure" career position, supposedly having less chronic stress at work. When devoting themselves to work, some women respondents reflected upon how not having children was not an active choice, neither was it something they especially regretted:

> I never really wanted to have children. Now when I'm over thirty and most friends have one or two, maybe I at times think that I'm missing out on something, but it was never something important, never something I've thought about.
>
> (Female middle manager in a B2B company, 30s, no children, Finland)

Stressful conditions at work often spill out into the private sphere, affecting the ability to recharge and engage in care responsibilities. Burnout was frequently spoken of in our interviews; they often felt they "barely made it":

> I'm just keeping my head above water.
>
> (Female top manager in a B2B company, 40s, one child, Australia)

To facilitate ambitious careers, regardless of having children or not, many companies have created a service model where employees get assistance for care-work that may otherwise be unpaid in their private spheres. This assistance is often made more attractive to employees that are more valuable to the company. It can include nannies for children, domestic cleaning, grocery shopping, cooking, possibly care for elderly parents – often provided by women from less privileged, ethnicised/racialised backgrounds – so enabling the "more valuable" employee to continue devoting themselves to work regardless of life phase and situation. In all its "helpfulness," it frees the "valuable employee" from care responsibilities, strengthening the "ideal worker" model and making it the norm in capitalist organisations, often outsourcing care to less privileged women. It is an unequal gendered, often ethnicised/racialised, model in itself. A more responsible way of organising work and care would be to acknowledge the need for a change in capitalist work cultures, introducing more equitable and sustainable ways of organising work and care throughout the life course, for all.

Conclusion

How work and care are unevenly distributed in different phases of life is a key question for social sustainability. This includes the structuring of boundaries between the private and the public realms, between work and care, as well as spatial, temporal, and other boundaries. Questions of work and care across life phases continue to be of major significance for the everyday lives of people and for employers and states. They underpin many wider, intersectional inequalities and discriminations, and are central for sustainable systems of production and reproduction in society.

For production and reproduction in society, both (paid) work and (paid and unpaid) care are vital. For a more sustainable society, work and care, or work/care, need to be more equally valued and distributed in organisations and society. Responsible organising within and around organisations means engaging with these persistent realities, indeed inequalities, at both strategic and everyday levels of organising, not left to the whims of individual managers and supervisors, nor as an occasional afterthought in organisations and organising.

References

Acker, J. (1990). Hierarchies, jobs, bodies: a theory of gendered organizations. *Gender & Society*, 4(2): 139–158. https://doi.org/10.1177/089124390004002002

Field, J. C. and Chan, X. W. (2018). Contemporary knowledge workers and the boundaryless work–life interface. *Frontiers in Psychology*, 9: 2414. https://doi.org/10.3389/fpsyg.2018.02414

Hearn, J. and Hobson, B. (2020). Gender, state and citizenships: challenges and dilemmas in feminist theorizing. In T. Janoski, C. de Leon, J. Misra and I. W. Martin (Eds.) *The New Handbook of Political Sociology*. Cambridge: Cambridge University Press, pp. 153–190. https://doi.org/10.1017/9781108147828

Hearn, J. and Parkin, W., with R. Howson and C. Niemistö (2021). *Age at Work: Ambiguous Boundaries of Organizations, Organizing and Ageing*. London: Sage. https://doi.org/10.1093/geroni/igx014

Lewis, S., Gambles, R. and Rapoport, R. (2007). The constraints of a 'work–life balance' approach: an international perspective. *The International Journal of Human Resource Management*, 18(3): 360–373. https://doi.org/10.1080/09585190601165577

Littig, B. and Griessler, E. (2005). Social sustainability: a catchword between political pragmatism and social theory. *International Journal of Sustainable Development*, 8: 65–79. https://nbn-resolving.org/urn:nbn:de:0168-ssoar-5491

Niemistö, C., Hearn, J. and Kehn, C. (2021a). Care and work matter: a social sustainability approach. In C. Binswanger and A. Zimmermann, A. (Eds.) *Transitioning to Gender Equality*. Book series *Transitioning to Sustainability*. Basel: MDPI, , pp. 179–195. https://doi.org/10.3390/books978-3-03897-867-1

Niemistö, C., Hearn, J., Kehn, C. and Tuori, A. (2021b). Career women and motherhood within the 'Finnish Dream': slow progress in professional knowledge-intensive organisations. *Work, Employment and Society*, 35(4): 696–715. https://doi.org/10.1177/0950017020987392

Pfau-Effinger, B. (2005). Welfare state policies and the development of care arrangements. *European Societies*, 7(2): 321–347. https://doi.org/10.1080/14616690500083592

Tronto, J. (1993). *Moral Boundaries: A Political Argument for an Ethic of Care*. New York: Routledge.

Tronto, J. (2013). *Caring Democracy: Markets, Equality, and Justice*. New York: New York University Press.

Truong, T-D. (1996). Gender, international migration and social reproduction. *Asian and Pacific Migration Journal*, 5(1): 27–52. https://doi.org/10.1177/011719689600500103

Part IV

Engaging with the nonhuman world

17 The nature–human dichotomy within disaster governance

Eija Meriläinen and Martin Fougère

Introduction

This chapter discusses how disaster governance practitioners based in Northern Finland articulate nature–human relations, and particularly how the nature–human dichotomy is present or challenged in their articulations of "hazards" and "disasters." Where a hazard is typically a phenomenon that causes disruption, a disaster refers to the hazard's aftermath unfolding over time, with an emphasis on negative impacts, particularly on a community or society (see e.g., Kelman, 2018). Amidst global environmental change, the frequency and intensity of many so-called "natural" and "human-induced" hazards are expected to increase. On the one hand, climate change contributes to "natural" hazards such as wildfires and floods. On the other hand, "human-induced" hazards such as industrial accidents grow more likely, as converting "nature" into resources becomes increasingly risky.

The categorisation of hazards into "natural" or "human-induced" is just one illustration of how disaster governance knowledge and practice tend to evoke a nature–human dichotomy. The dichotomy is present in how everything from causality to suffering in disasters is made sense of. While hazards might be labelled "natural," human activity plays a central role in how most hazards evolve into disasters (Kelman, 2018). This is often misleadingly made sense of through the dichotomy, with a natural hazard understood to causally affect a society which then produces a disaster (Oliver-Smith, 2013), rather than the causes and effects being seen as entangled.

We show that while the nature–human dichotomy is central to disaster governance, there are tensions between how literature and frameworks articulate nature–human relations, and how the practitioners "on the ground" conceptualise them from their various subject positions. The chapter draws attention to the practitioners of disaster governance, who

DOI: 10.4324/9781003229728-21

pragmatically organise disaster preparedness, prevention, and response in the most responsible ways possible. Our aim is to question whether thinking premised on a nature–human dichotomy is useful for disaster governance.

The chapter's strength and limitation lie in that it is focused on actors at the interface of the modern state apparatus and local perspectives. This closeness to the state and its dominant language does not produce the most radical articulations, but it shows how the dichotomy operates in contemporary organising. The chapter is particularly relevant to the United Nations Sustainable Development Goals (SDGs) 13 and 15 on climate action and life on land. The nature–human dichotomy pervades the formulation of the SDGs, and the chapter supports critical reflection on the usefulness of the dichotomy in striving to address sustainability challenges.

The nature–human dichotomy in disaster governance

The concept of "nature," wedged apart from the social realm of humans, has been central to the project of Enlightenment. The nature–human dichotomy is embedded in contemporary perspectives on organising. Social sciences also typically approach humans as separate from nature, with nature acting as the backdrop of human agency. Human beings are seen to shape history and nature, while nature is subject to laws discussed in the "natural sciences" (Kagan, 2009). Over the past decades, however, different thinkers from science studies have increasingly protested what they see as an artificial line drawn between humans and nature (see e.g., Haraway, 2016; Latour, 2004).

The devastating impact of human activities on Earth's webs of life has been a key motivation for scientific scrutiny on the nature–human dichotomy. The dichotomy has served to justify the exploitation of nature for the benefit of humans (Moore, 2017) and obscure the extent to which human influence shapes the Earth and its processes (Head, 2008). The nature–human dichotomy is pervasive in modern forms of organising, from how states manage their territories to how companies use "natural resources." Problematising the dichotomy can help imagine alternative and responsible ways of organising (Wright et al., 2018).

We distinguish between nature–human and nature–society relations. We refer to the nature–human dichotomy as the broad umbrella concept that ranges across scales, from a species perspective to individual-level relations. Meanwhile, the nature–society dichotomy relates more specifically to how societies associated with modern states relate to nature.

The nature–human dichotomy is very much present in disaster governance, as well as in the closely related set of academic studies called "disaster studies." Disasters comprise the devastating impacts that follow from hazards and these are typically described as impacts on humans: how many human lives were lost and how much rebuilding infrastructure will cost. This is particularly the case when the disaster can be traced back to a "natural" hazard. While "nature" – from ecosystems to pets – and its interface with "humans" might be severely affected as a result of the hazard (Kelman, 2021), the impacts on "nature," in disaster studies, are typically translated into indirect impacts on humans (e.g., loss of livelihood), or thought of as mostly natural (e.g., fires as part of ecosystem renewal). The nature–human dichotomy is thus strongly embedded into how hazards and disasters are made sense of. Nature and humans/society are treated as two separate entities that have impacts on each other rather than seen as constituting one assemblage, with constant, dynamic entanglements.

One key deployer of the nature–human dichotomy is the modern state. States are generally understood as having a duty to protect their citizens, and disaster governance frameworks are adopted on state-level. National and local governments remain central actors in disaster governance, even if with neoliberalism the responsibility and resources for disaster governance have become increasingly dispersed (Meriläinen, 2020). States *ideally* coordinate disaster governance efforts over time, represent the interests of the populations within their borders, and can arbitrate on matters of justice and equality. It is for this reason that the chapter zooms in on the interface between the modern state and local concerns.

The nature–human dichotomy in Northern Finnish disaster governance

"Modernity" arrived to what is now labelled as Finland fairly recently, with non-dichotomous nature–human understandings and relations lingering on in the practices of everyday life (Helsti et al., 2006). While tourists and thinkers alike have imagined particularly the Northern natures as untouched by humans, the local views do not similarly separate humans from nature (Komu, 2019; Lehtinen, 2006). Articulations of non-dichotomous nature–human relations associate particularly with the Sámi community (Toivanen & Fabritius, 2020). Yet, despite the slow encroachment of modernity to Northern Finland, colonising imperial and state politics have shaped the region over hundreds of years with varying intensities. This has changed not only the local "natures," but also livelihoods and how the humans do and can relate to the rest of "nature."

Contemporarily, the modern Finnish state is very much present in Northern Finland, including in matters of disaster governance. The Finnish state does not have a central coordinating disaster governance agency. Instead, disaster governance is organised based on the hazard type. While the state apparatus is central to disaster governance in Finland, responsibility is dispersed across society, and volunteer organisations and companies are also involved in this governance effort (Pilli-Sihvola et al., 2018). This draws various organisations' disaster governance under the umbrella of the state-led frameworks, but it also creates a possibility for different understandings and articulations of disaster governance across the actors.

Our empirical illustration is based on interviews with disaster governance practitioners in Northern Finland. Below we discuss how the practitioners articulate relationships between humans and nature in the context of disaster governance.

In their professional roles as part of organisations involved in disaster governance, the practitioners reproduce a nature–human dichotomy in many ways, specifically by separating contemporary society from nature. Although nature itself is not seen as an obvious direct threat to humans, nature is constructed by the practitioners as a threat to society. When nature's elements – from a wildfire to a moose – clash with the infrastructures of contemporary society, nature turns into a threat. As one practitioner notes, most "natural" disasters are brought about by the societies themselves, but in technical terms, "we do have lakes that are killing people a lot, ultimately, so that is quite surprising. And it is the same notion as the moose being the most dangerous animal, as it kills most in traffic. Statistically." What this implies is that within disaster governance as construed by the Finnish state and Finnish professionals, nature as cause on the one hand and society as that which is affected by disasters on the other, tend to be framed as two separate entities.

However, in their personal views, the practitioners make a far less clear-cut separation between nature and humans, seeing themselves as having a close personal relationship to nature and often acknowledging the tension with their professional relationship to nature. One practitioner emphasises their personal love for Northern Finnish nature, but adds that in their work, nature is a source of burdens and worries which poses risks to humans. For another practitioner, nature is casually associated with being outdoors and a sense of immersion, being at one with nature, but professionally they "immediately see a threat" in nature. The tensions between subject positions are also clear in another practitioner's shifts between describing "nature as client" and "nature as subject in its own right."

This notion of nature's subjecthood is present in how nature is portrayed as an all-powerful organiser whose agency has to be understood:

> nature takes care of forest fires, organises forest fires, puts down forest fires, burns down cities if need be, organises the wind, organises the corona, so that is, it is nature after all, that has all this, humans just try to live with it.

Nature has a way of sorting things out so that they work, so even when trying to prevent adverse impacts on humans through disaster governance, humans should "make use of nature's capacities so that one does not harm the functioning" of nature, according to yet another practitioner. This implies that while the disaster governance mandate is to reduce the impacts of disasters on society, the actions undertaken should be in line with nature.

Despite nature's agency, the values and practices of contemporary society have in effect placed nature in a corner, where its powers and processes can be turned against itself. Wildfires serve as an example here. Contemporary society often prioritises fire suppression, foregrounding the commercial value of nature. For nature itself, a wildfire can be part of natural renewal; as one practitioner notes: "presumably it has happened for time immemorial – for thousands of years – that a lightning has struck a tree." Yet, in many contemporary instances, the cause of the wildfire is a cigarette stump or a campfire, and the natural renewal of the forest cannot keep up with the fires sparked. Another practitioner points out that even natural hazards "are almost always caused by humans, so are they then philosophically speaking natural disasters [sic] or are they impacts caused by humans on nature?"

Conclusion

This chapter shows that disaster governance frameworks and organising rely on the nature–human/society dichotomy in making sense of hazards and disasters, even if the practitioners acknowledge the fundamental entanglement of humans and nature. Indeed, the practitioners we interviewed highlight a difference between their personal accounts and their professional views. The ways in which a "disaster" relates to nature–human and nature–society relationships depends on which subject position they speak from. When the practitioners relate to nature in their personal accounts, *nature* and *human* can be entangled. However, in their professional accounts, it is the nature–society relationship that becomes pronounced, with modern *society* appearing to stand apart from nature. For the practitioners, society is associated with modern infrastructure, technocratic frameworks, and a professional duty to think in terms of economic impacts. Many, if not most, disasters are seen as caused by society, with the causality of impacts flowing through nature more broadly, to humans as part of it. If it was not for the excesses of modern society, hazards would not be disastrous to nature, but part of its renewal.

The tensions in how nature–human/society relations are expressed lead us to some critical reflections about sustainable development and the mode of intervention based on the SDGs. In the SDGs (e.g., SDGs 13 and 15) humans are given an agentic role in correcting issues that are, if not entirely attributed to nature, assumed to characterise a "new normal" of hazardous "natural" phenomena which are to be tackled by humans. By assuming that humans can isolate these phenomena as objects of their corrective interventions, the SDG vision runs the risk of not understanding the entanglements of the ("productive" and "corrective") human activities with the "natural" phenomena. We argue that it is important to challenge this dichotomous way of thinking about nature–human relations. It is not that governance practitioners necessarily believe humans are estranged or independent from nature, the problem lies in the professional frameworks that are used to abstract nature and society as two fully separate spheres.

Acknowledgements

This research was supported through the Belmont Forum by the UK's Natural Environment Research Council (grant number: NE/T013656/1), as well as with scholarships from Hanken Support Foundation and Foundation for Economic Education in Finland.

References

Haraway, D. J. (2016). *Staying with the Trouble: Making Kin in the Chthulucene*. Duke University Press Books.

Head, L. (2008). Is the concept of human impacts past its use-by date? *The Holocene*, *18*(3), 373–377. https://doi.org/10.1177/0959683607087927

Helsti, H., Stark, L., & Tuomaala, S. (2006). *Modernisaatio ja kansan kokemus Suomessa 1860-1960*. Suomalaisen Kirjallisuuden Seura. https://researchportal.helsinki.fi/en/publications/modernisaatio-ja-kansan-kokemus-suomessa-1860-1960

Kagan, J. (2009). *The Three Cultures: Natural Sciences, Social Sciences, and the Humanities in the 21st Century.* Cambridge University Press. https://doi.org/10.1017/CBO9780511576638

Kelman, I. (2018). Lost for words amongst disaster risk science vocabulary? *International Journal of Disaster Risk Science, 9*(3), 281–291. https://doi.org/10.1007/s13753-018-0188-3

Kelman, I. (2021). Categorising animals and habitats in disaster-related activities. *The Australian Journal of Emergency Management, 36*(3), 57–62. https://doi.org/10.3316/informit.947840633094167

Komu, T. (2019). Dreams of treasures and dreams of wilderness – engaging with the beyond-the-rational in extractive industries in northern Fennoscandia. *The Polar Journal, 9*(1), 113–132. https://doi.org/10.1080/2154896X.2019.1618556

Latour, B. (2004). *Politics of Nature: How to Bring the Sciences into Democracy.* Harvard University Press.

Lehtinen, A. A. (2006). *Postcolonialism, Multitude, and the Politics of Nature: On the Changing Geographies of the European North.* UPA.

Meriläinen, E. (2020). *Urban Disaster Governance: Resilience and Rights in the Unequal City.* Hanken School of Economics. https://helda.helsinki.fi/dhanken/handle/10227/320855

Moore, J. W. (2017). The Capitalocene, Part I: On the nature and origins of our ecological crisis. *The Journal of Peasant Studies, 44*(3), 594–630. https://doi.org/10.1080/03066150.2016.1235036

Oliver-Smith, A. (2013). A matter of choice. *International Journal of Disaster Risk Reduction, 3*, 1–3. https://doi.org/10.1016/j.ijdrr.2012.12.001

Pilli-Sihvola, K., Harjanne, A., & Haavisto, R. (2018). Adaptation by the least vulnerable: Managing climate and disaster risks in Finland. *International Journal of Disaster Risk Reduction, 31*, 1266–1275. https://doi.org/10.1016/j.ijdrr.2017.12.004

Toivanen, R., & Fabritius, N. (2020). Arctic youth transcending notions of 'culture' and 'nature': Emancipative discourses of place for cultural sustainability. *Current Opinion in Environmental Sustainability, 43*, 58–64. https://doi.org/10.1016/j.cosust.2020.02.003

Wright, C., Nyberg, D., Rickards, L., & Freund, J. (2018). Organizing in the Anthropocene. *Organization, 25*(4), 455–471. https://doi.org/10.1177/1350508418779649

18 Humans and water

The problem(s) with affordability

Linda Annala Tesfaye, Martin Fougère, and Yewondwossen Tesfaye

Introduction

This chapter discusses social inequalities resulting from humans striving to govern, control, and manage water through technological, political, and economic forms of organising. Contemporary depictions of global water crises and depleting groundwater levels create powerful imaginaries of water as an increasingly scarce substance. Approaching water merely through a scarcity discourse is simplistic, since there is enough water on this planet for all. However, water sources are becoming increasingly contaminated, salinated, or dried up largely due to industrial and agricultural uses. These processes affect domestic access to drinking water as well, and water may not be accessible when and where people need it. Large inequalities persist in terms of accessing clean water on a global scale: 844 million individuals do not have access to basic drinking water. One of the United Nations Sustainable Development Goals (SDGs), SDG 6, aims to achieve access to safe and affordable drinking water for everyone. In this chapter, we engage critically with the concept of "affordability" and how it has deradicalised the discourse on human right to water at different scales.

The essentiality of water as a life-sustaining substance continues to press societies to govern and control water. Different political, technological, and economic forms of organising have developed to solve water problems. This chapter elucidates how private innovations in the context of drinking water governance shift public responsibility into the realm of private responsibility, and what kinds of consequences this has for unequal access to drinking water. Using examples from Ethiopia and India, we question the responsibility of current ways of organising water governance and argue for new ways of organising.

DOI: 10.4324/9781003229728-22

Human right to water?

The UN General Assembly's resolution in 2010 established that "the human right to safe drinking water entitles everyone, without discrimination, to have access to sufficient, safe, acceptable, physically accessible and affordable water for personal and domestic use..." (UN, 2010). The resolution resulted from resistance to the 1992 Dublin Statement – a preparatory agenda to the Earth Summit organised in Rio de Janeiro in 1992 – according to which:

> Water has an economic value in all its competing uses and should be recognised as an economic good. Within this principle, it is vital to recognise first the basic right of all human beings to have access to clean water and sanitation at an affordable price. (ICWE, 1992)

The highly contested Dublin Statement paved the way for putting a price tag on water and pushed water governance policies in many parts of the world towards the active involvement of the private sector in the provision of water. As the power of resisting voices grew stronger and several privatisation efforts of public water utilities failed (e.g., in Bolivia and Indonesia), water became defined as a human right as per the UN resolution – supposedly in opposition to the Dublin Statement.

We understand "human right to water" as a discourse that shapes and is shaped by social practices at various levels. Civil society actors and activists have used the human right to water discourse and the subsequent UN resolution to prevent clean and safe water from becoming a profit-making commodity accessible only for those who can afford prices based on full cost recovery (Bakker, 2007). In theory, governments have the duty to protect and fulfil the right to water, although in practice the resolution has not yielded transformational change.

On the other hand, the human right to water discourse has invited solutions that rely on the concept of affordability, shifting the focus from an absolute human right to access to affordable water. We argue that the emphasis on "affordability" within the human right to water discourse (as well as in SDG 6), while making it possible for activists to appeal to lower prices (Yates & Harris, 2018), makes the discourse compatible with private, market-led solutions to accessing water. It further suggests at least three things: (1) water has an economic value and cannot be exchanged completely for free, (2) water is framed as a matter of "consumer choice" whether buying affordable water solutions is to be prioritised over other expenses, and (3) access to water is a technical issue that can be solved simplistically by rendering it "afford-able enough" for all. While affordability is mentioned in SDG 6 as an enabling attribute in achieving universal and equitable access to safe drinking water for all, we criticise its tendencies of shifting the political questions of accessing drinking water into the economic realm.

Deployment of the deradicalised human right to water discourse

In the following examples, we show how privatisation and unequal access to water become veiled in the language of affordability and thus deradicalise the human right to water discourse on different scales: macro, meso, and micro.

Macro-policy discourse: dominant policy networks and SDG 6

Macro-level water discourses result from the vested interests of dominant private actors, corporate philanthropies, multilateral organisations, and national governments of the Global North in the governance of water in general and the formulation of the SDGs in particular (Cummings et al., 2017). Interestingly, affordability was not mentioned in relation to access to water in the UN Millennium Development Goals (MDGs), which guided global development policy from 2000 to 2015, when they were replaced by the SDGs. It was only through the UN Resolution and later the SDGs that the two approaches of "access to water" and "water as an economic resource" became reconciled through "afford-able water."

Such a merging of perspectives, however, did not happen without long-term discursive work by several actors, such as the transnational policy network World Business Council for Sustainable Development (WBCSD). The WBCSD's influential report "Water for the Poor" in 2002 set a powerful "win-win-win" political rationality envisaging a con-sensual approach of simultaneously fulfilling the needs of corporations, public institutions, and the poor in terms of water provision. The poor would benefit from affordable prices, as they were already paying dis-proportionate prices for accessing poor quality water, governments would benefit from providing access to water to their underserved citi-zens, and corporations would benefit through profits.

On the macro-level, the focus on affordability transforms a poten-tially radical argument for making water a fundamental human right into a project of facilitating the development of "huge employment and sales opportunities for large and small businesses alike" (WBCSD, 2002, p. 8).

Meso-initiatives on affordable water innovations in Ethiopia

Macro-level water discourses are translated to the meso-level in different parts of the Global South. We illustrate this through the case of an entrepreneurial initiative on mobilising water innovations in Ethiopia. In line with the Ethiopian government's strategy of scaling up business incubation centres as well as wider neoliberal reforms of encouraging youth to become risk-taking entrepreneurs (Dolan & Rajak, 2016), two actors, Iceaddis and Aqua for All, have together established an innovation incubation programme in the capital city Addis Abeba directed specifically at developing water innovations.

Iceaddis is Ethiopia's first innovation hub and tech start-up incubator whereas Aqua for All is a global not-for-profit organisation that provides entrepreneurial financing through the global network Sanitation and Water Entrepreneurship Pact. Within their programme, inclusiveness and revenue models are tied together, promoting affordability as the central tenet of water innovations. However, their effort to construct "business opportunities" for entrepreneurial water innovations runs the risk of promising too much in an industry where it remains difficult to find a balance between profit and inclusive access (Swyngedouw, 2013). Many entrepreneurs struggle to make profit as water innovations tend to be politicised and challenging to scale up (Daniell et al., 2014). When an innovation does succeed in being profitable, it may be at the cost of access of the marginalised people.

On the meso-level, the quest for affordability is built on a largely illusory win-win promise between profit opportunities for small entrepreneurs and inclusive, "affordable" access to water. However, the outcomes tend to be suboptimal from both the business and the access perspectives.

Micro-reception of water innovation in a rural village in India

Macro-level water discourses also have material and ideological impacts on the micro-level of local communities. We illustrate this through an example of the reception of water innovation in Peeth, a drought-prone rural village in Rajasthan, India (Tesfaye Gemechu, 2018). In 2012, the first private supply was introduced by the company Sarvajal Waters to supply "safe and affordable drinking water." Sarvajal's approach constituted an innovative mechanism which combined a simple, desalinating water purification technology with an entrepreneurial service delivery modality. This approach strived to achieve affordability through a cheap price. However, after four years of implementation, Sarvajal delivered water to only 15 per cent of Peeth's households.

Our example shows that affordability does not seem to be the most decisive reason for (non)adoption of "cleaner" water solutions (Tesfaye Gemechu, 2018). Prioritising other areas of life, most households wished to stick to the public "unsafe," but cheaper water service – finding Sarvajal's "safe" product outside of their priority domain. The discourse of affordability constructs neoliberal, rational water users responsible for self-care – those who enrol to Sarvajal's safe and affordable water service – in opposition to irresponsible water users who lack the economic and basic rationality of self-care. Such subjectivities (re) produce differences among the households and construct inequalities in terms of access to clean water.

On the micro-level, a focus on affordability leads to "responsibilisation" of the poor. The moral burden of making the right consumption choice – selecting safe water provided at an "affordable" price – is transferred to the users. In this logic of affordability, responsibility for unequal access to water falls on the end user.

Conclusion

We argue that the "human right to water" discourse is losing its radical potential through the increased focus on affordability. The transformation of the discourse into a water privatisation-compatible project through the concept of affordability is of great concern from the perspective of equal access to water for people across the world. With our examples from Ethiopia and India, we have shown how the concept of affordability has been crucial in shaping the connection between the human right to water discourse and private technology in providing access to drinking water. The macro-level discourse of affordability has resulted in a consequent systematisation of initiatives to boost "water innovation" and entrepreneurial drives in relation to water in the Global South. These initiatives have consequences for how local communities can access drinking water (SDG 6) and they have produced inequalities (SDG 10) between households through increasing private water costs.

Goldman (2007) discusses how specific organisations dominate the transnational production and circulation of knowledge around water. This is problematic as a top-down discourse yields a tendency to suffocate community-level voices. Responsible organising of water governance requires that the needs of the communities on their own terms be understood and legitimised. Ideally, the SDGs should help in hearing and understanding communal voices. However, the vaguely operationalised and monitored concept of affordability within SDG 6 instead seems to keep communities exposed to the neoliberal logics of individualisation and responsibilisation that private initiatives providing access to affordable water produce.

Acknowledgements

This work has been supported by the Foundation for Economic Education in Finland (grant number: 200046) and Hanken Support Foundation.

References

Bakker, K. (2007). The "commons" versus the "commodity": Alter-globalization, anti-privatization and the human right to water in the global south. *Antipode*, 39(3), 430–455, https://doi.org/10.1111/j.1467-8330.2007.00534.x

Cummings, S., Regeer, B., de Haan, L., Zweekhorst, M. and Bunders, J. (2017). Critical discourse analysis of perspectives on knowledge and the knowledge society within the Sustainable Development Goals. *Development Policy Review*, 36, 727–742, https://doi.org/10.1111/dpr.12296

Daniell, K., Coombes, P. and White, I. (2014). Politics of innovation in multilevel water governance systems. *Journal of Hydrology*, 519, Part C, 2415–2435, https://doi.org/10.1016/j.jhydrol.2014.08.058

Dolan, C. and Rajak, D. (2016). Remaking Africa's informal economies: Youth, entrepreneurship and the promise of inclusion at the bottom of the pyramid. *The Journal of Development Studies*, 52(4), 514–529, http://dx.doi.org/10.1080/00220388.2015.1126249

Goldman, M. (2007). How "Water for All!" policy became hegemonic: The power of the World Bank and its transnational policy networks. *Geoforum*, 38(5), 786–800, https://doi.org/10.1016/j.geoforum.2005.10.008

ICWE (1992). The Dublin Statement on Water and Sustainable Development. www.gdrc.org/uem/water/dublin-statement.html (accessed 16 February 2022).

Swyngedouw, E. (2013). UN water report 2012: Depoliticizing water. *Development and Change*, 44(3), 823–835, https://doi.org/10.1111/dech.12033

Tesfaye Gemechu, Y. (2018). On water users' repertoire: Market rationality and governmentality in Peeth village's water supply, Rajasthan (India). *Geoforum*, 94, 33–40, https://doi.org/10.1016/j.geoforum.2018.06.001

UN (2010). United Nations. The human right to water and sanitation: Resolution/Adopted by the General Assembly.

WBCSD (2002). Water for the Poor. World Business Council for Sustainable Development. http://docs.wbcsd.org/2002/08/WaterForThePoor.pdf (accessed 6 December 2021)

Yates, J. S., and Harris, L. M. (2018). Hybrid regulatory landscapes: The human right to water, variegated neoliberal water governance, and policy transfer in Cape Town, South Africa, and Accra, Ghana. *World Development*, 110, 75–87, https://doi.org/10.1016/j.worlddev.2018.05.021

19 Human and nonhuman animals in a posthuman reality

Accreditation schemes as voice?

Linda Tallberg and Janne Tienari

Introduction

This chapter argues that nonhuman animal interests are often silenced in the discourse of sustainable development. We explore the challenges and potential for including nonhuman animal (hereafter "animal") voice in the marketplace through accreditation schemes for animal "cruelty-free" products run by animal protection organisations for consumer goods businesses. Ethical treatment of animals is still missing in most public and private debates, despite the significant role animals play in our societies and lives. Animals are our companions and colleagues. Yet, they are often instrumentalised for their bodies as food, laboratory testing, clothing, and entertainment.

In key arenas of promoting responsibility through global change, such as the United Nations Sustainable Development Goals (SDGs), animal interests remain predominantly silenced. A limiting agenda for responsible societal and industry change is thus retained. How can there be sustainability without recognising the interconnectivity of human-nonhuman wellbeing in planetary health? Human-animal interactions and coexistence must be recognised as upholding human relational duties and moral responsibilities (Donaldson & Kymlicka, 2011). As human animals, we are intimately connected as part of a natural system which is out of balance due to human activities. For example, to feed an increasingly growing human population, our inefficient food systems slaughter at least 88 billion land-based and 1–3 trillion aquatic animals annually, most of whose upkeep comes at a human cost. For example, animals eat grains that could instead be used as human nourishment. Animals suffer intensely during their short, intensified lives as they are used as breeding machines for their offspring or for their body parts and excretions. The detrimental effects of mistreating animals are connected to human suffering as biodiversity

DOI: 10.4324/9781003229728-23

loss, deforestation, and climate change impact the current and future wellbeing of humans.

Injustice to animals is a blind spot in the SDGs, which have yet to recognise sustainable development as an interspecies agenda with intimate interconnections between humans and animals, rather than grouping animals into the generalised categories of "life below water" (SDG 14) and "life on land" (SDG 15). These do not consider large polluters or systems of suffering such as animal agriculture in a serious manner. Nonhuman life remains largely separate from economic, health, societal, and justice agendas. The relative disregard of nonhumans in SDGs such as "zero hunger" (SDG 2), "good health and wellbeing" (SDG 3) "reduced inequalities" (SDG 10) and, most prominently, "responsible consumption and production" (SDG 12) retains limited thinking of separating the development of human wellbeing from the nonhuman world.

To organise human interaction with animals in more responsible ways requires that societies put pressure on industries to assume moral duties hitherto largely evaded in the limited focus on economic and social gains (Ergene et al., 2021; Tallberg et al., 2022). Differently from many Indigenous relational ontologies (see Chapters 4 and 20), the Western way of life has been slow to recognise and respect the interconnected aspects of planetary life and to assume responsibility beyond profit and human wellbeing, thereby accelerating the environmental and climate crisis. The representation of animal voice is traditionally missing in decision-making arenas such as the marketplace. We use a posthuman affirmative ethical perspective to analyse whether market-based accreditation schemes could be a way forward in highlighting nonhuman animal interests.

Posthuman affirmative ethics in business

Posthumanism recognises that animals are not passive objects but active subjects and agents that are affected by and affecting interactions with humans (Braidotti, 2019). The posthuman agenda of including animal voice into public awareness can be thought of in terms of interspecies sustainability and ethics (Probyn-Rapsey et al., 2016) whereby we recognise our mutual dependency. An interspecies ethics is part of recognising our posthuman reality and shifting awareness to consider animal interests in influential arenas. For example, our educational institutions such as business schools are important spaces to explore posthuman affirmative values and potentially translating them for companies to consider (Tallberg et al., 2022). But how can businesses communicate such values to consumers? Especially in times of "greenwashing" practices of companies to market a sustainable and ethical agenda (see Kopina, 2021), transparency is key in understanding how animals can be helped and their voices and interests heard.

According to Rosi Braidotti (2019, p. 156), affirmative ethics can be defined as:

> a collective practice of constructing social horizons of hope, in response to the flagrant injustices, the perpetrations of old hierarchies and new forms of domination…in favour of *zoe*/geo/techno [nonhuman] relations, and to assess their ability to process pain and construct an ethical subjectivity worthy of our times.

In business and industry practices, posthuman affirmative ethics necessitates shifts in humancentric thinking to highlight exploitative practices in our interactions with animals in order to create more positive mutual futures (Sayers et al., 2021; Tallberg et al., 2022). This requires a heightened sense of "response-ability" and relational understanding of equality and justice to, with, and for nonhuman life (Braidotti, 2019; Sayers et al., 2021).

Challenges and opportunities in accreditation schemes

Different products in the marketplace may be highlighted as "sustainable" through accreditation schemes by animal protection organisations. We explore whether animal voice is transmitted through accreditation schemes of animal protection organisations and consider if these help to work on a posthuman affirmative ethical approach in the marketplace.

Animal protection organisations have to date most clearly acted as the "spokespersons" of animal interests. Consumers increasingly rely on information by such monitoring organisations to impart business practices and values for informed consumption choices, whether in the context of the local supermarket or online in global marketplaces. As such, these organisations are seen to speak on behalf of animals in spaces often without direct live animal contact. We discuss two examples of accreditation schemes. The first example, RSPCA Australia, is from a country that has one of the most ingrained farmed animal agriculture traditions in the world along with economic interests predominantly dominating the environmental and nonhuman societal discourse. Our second example is a global accreditation scheme, PETA-approved, whose products can be found world-wide.

Animal welfare and the RSPCA-approved farming scheme

According to the animal welfare organisation RSPCA Australia, their accreditation scheme focuses on improving the welfare standards for animals in Australian intense animal agriculture industries (chicken, layer hens, pigs, salmon, dairy calves, and turkey). They report that at least 2 billion farm animals have "better" welfare due to their scheme, which started in 1996 and focuses on setting a welfare standard for a "better quality of life" for farmed animals "beyond current legal requirements" while being "commercially viable" (see https://rspcaa pproved.org.au/about). An RSPCA assessor makes 2–4 yearly on-site visits along with reviewing production information between visits to check whether farms uphold RSPCA welfare standards.

If standards hold in practice throughout farm operations, it seems that RSPCA-approved farms may have slightly better living conditions for animals than those who do not. However, the scheme mainly benefits animal production companies in their brand management and marketing through the stamp of approval from a societally influential animal welfare organisation, who in return receives royalties from the scheme participants. Hence, from an animal voice perspective, while offering slightly improved animal welfare, the scheme supports the con-tinuation and legitimisation of practices that kill and exploit animals. Animal interests are secondary to commercial interests. This accredit-ation scheme also does nothing to consider the environmental impact of animal agriculture (Poore & Nemechek, 2018). Viewed through a posthuman affirmative ethical lens, RSPCA Australia adopts a humancentric agenda of instrumentalising animals most vulnerable, i.e., in food systems, by not challenging traditional "Aussie" mascu-line narratives of meat-eating (see Taylor et al., 2022), which invariably negatively affects both animal and human wellbeing.

Animal voice in PETA-approved schemes

The global animal rights organisation PETA runs several accreditation schemes. Since 1987, PETA has collaborated with companies in sectors that traditionally have relied on animal testing, such as cosmetics, personal care, and household goods, with the global schemes "animal test-free" and "animal test-free and vegan." Here, companies commit to never test on animals and, in the latter, to be free of animal-derived ingredients (and, thus, cruelty-free). There is also the "PETA's Global Beauty Without Bunnies" scheme that offers an online database and "Bunny free" app for "conscientious shoppers" looking for cruelty-free humane products. The newest scheme, "PETA Approved Vegan," includes clothing, accessories, furniture, home décor, and companion animal food made from vegan alternatives.

From a posthuman affirmative ethical lens, the PETA schemes help animal interests in a range of industries by eliminating animals' physical involvement in production practices and assisting humans in aligning their consumption choices with values that support interspecies ethical choices, at least to avoid harming animals in production. The schemes also consider the environmental effects of the products. Over 1,000 companies are "PETA Approved Vegan." This suggests that the scheme holds an influential position. However, as this is a self-reporting accreditation assessed by PETA (as the RSPCA scheme, based on a fee), there can be some issues related to monitoring. In lieu of other accreditations, the PETA schemes give confidence to consumers that the companies involved recognise that "animals are not ours to experiment on, eat, wear, use for entertainment, or abuse in any other way" (PETA, 2021). Hence, it seems that animal voice is represented in the PETA schemes as the main purpose is to alleviate animal suffering through offering consumers options that support an ethical treatment of animals.

Conclusion

Transformative action is needed on individual, organisational, societal, and global levels to respond to and change detrimental human behaviour that exploits the nonhuman world – for its own sake, but also in recognition of human wellbeing being dependent on the wellbeing of other planetary life. This is our posthuman reality where we must recognise our interconnectivity. Posthuman affirmative ethics (Braidotti, 2019; Sayers et al., 2021) supports shifting responsibility and sustainability beyond limited humancentric interests to include nonhuman life such as animals. Businesses are key societal actors, and they are needed to create positive change towards responsible organising that includes nonhuman animals.

However, a core difficulty is how animal interests can be voiced in the marketplace. This is due to the often hidden and complex industrial production systems and supply chains. In this chapter, we have examined two different examples of animal protection accreditation schemes and considered whether such measures could represent animal voice in the marketplace. We suggest that more public awareness is needed about production and consumption practices that involve animals, and recognition of whose interests are foremost considered in different schemes. More radical measures are needed for more affirmative ethical marketplaces to support interspecies sustainability on our planet. Such action can include behavioural modification-actions similar to tobacco labels or a sizable tax on animal-derived products. Simply avoiding companies and products that use animals supports an agenda for more sustainable and ethical human behaviours. Hence, it could be argued that PETA-approved schemes foremost uphold animal interests (and thus voice in the marketplace) whereas the RSPCA scheme is limited by upholding humancentric notions of animals-as-food. Analysing underlying motives behind actions labelled as "sustainable" or "responsible" translates similarly to deeper understanding of what can support voices that are traditionally marginalised and silenced.

Taking nonhuman interests more seriously is crucial for responsibly organising our societies into mutually positive futures for all planetary life. This includes reimagining business schools and theories for animal inclusivity (Tallberg et al., 2021). Not considering the entangled nature of our posthuman reality comes at a great cost to the future of humanity based on our unethical treatment of nonhuman life. As the SDGs represent a global action agenda for sustainable development and responsible organising, we ask: how are nonhuman interests covered in such "development"? Whose interests are included in our global agendas and whose are silenced? We argue that posthuman understanding is needed in global agendas and in the actions of key players such as business and industry. This could mean, for example, reformulating the SDGs from a posthuman affirmative ethical lens, which supports both human and nonhuman interests (such as the PETA accreditation example offers), rather than outdated commercial interests that do little to attend to our sustainability challenges at their root. Exploitation of the nonhuman world is a fundamental problem of our times. Listening to animal voices is a capability we must all learn if we wish to continue to share this planet with other nonhuman life.

References

Braidotti, R. (2019). *Posthuman knowledge*. Cambridge: Polity Press.

Donaldson, S. & Kymlicka, W. (2011). *Zoopolis: A political theory of animal rights*. Oxford: Oxford University Press.

Ergene, S., Banerjee, S. B., & Hoffman, A. J. (2021). (Un)Sustainability and Organization Studies: Towards a Radical Engagement. *Organization Studies*, 42(8): 1319–1335. https://doi.org/10.1177/0170840620937892

Kopina, H. (2021). Towards Ecological Management: Identifying Barriers and Opportunities in Transition from Linear to Circular Economy. *Philosophy of Management*, 20: 5–19. https://doi.org/10.1007/s40926-019-00108-x

PETA (2021). 'PETA-Approved Vegan' Logo. Available from www.peta.org/living/personal-care fashion/peta-approved-vegan-logo/

Poore, J. & Nemecek, T. (2018). Reducing Food's Environmental Impacts Through Producers and Consumers. *Science*, 360(6390): 987–992. https://doi.org/10.1126/science.aaq0216

Probyn-Rapsey, F., Donaldson, S., Ioannides, G., Lea, T., et al., (2016). A Sustainable Campus: The Sydney Declaration on Interspecies Sustainability. *Animal Studies Journal*, 5(1): 110–151. https://ro.uow.edu.au/asj/vol5/iss1/8

Sayers, J., Martin, L., & Bell, E. (2021). Posthuman Affirmative Business Ethics: Reimagining Human–Animal Relations Through Speculative Fiction. Journal of Business Ethics. https://doi.org/10.1007/s10551-021-04801-8

Tallberg, L., García-Rosell, J. C., & Haanpää, M. (2021). Human–Animal Relations in Business and Society: Advancing the Feminist Interpretation of Stakeholder Theory. *Journal of Business Ethics*. https://doi.org/10.1007/s10551-021-04840-1

Tallberg, L., Välikangas, L., & Hamilton, L. (2022). Animal Activism in the Business School: Using Fierce Compassion for Teaching Critical and Positive Perspectives. *Management Learning*, 53(1): 55–75. https://doi.org/10.1177/13505076211044612

Taylor, N., Fraser, H., Stekelenburg, N., & King, J. (2022). Barbaric, feral or moral? Stereotypical dairy farmer and vegan discourses on the business of animal consumption. In Tallberg, L. and Hamilton, L. (Eds.), *The Oxford handbook of animal organisation studies*. Oxford: Oxford University Press.

20 Ontological multiplicity

Responsible organising in defence of life

Maria Ehrnström-Fuentes and
Tiina Jääskeläinen

Introduction

This chapter argues for the need to account for multiple ontologies in responsible organising on the land. Many current debates on responsible organising lie within the boundaries of the modern ontology, which constructs a particular kind of world based on the assumptions that humans are separate from nature, time is linear, and (some) humans are superior to other humans and natures (Blaser, 2010). These assumptions about "the world" influence what kind of organising activities, and relations to nonhumans (e.g., rivers, mountains, animals) are considered legitimate (what is the "right" thing to do), responsible (what is "good" organisational conduct), and sustainable (what are the social and ecological impacts). For example, corporations in natural resource-based industries such as mining and forestry rely on access to land from which they can extract resources. However, the same land may be used by local community actors for fishing or hunting or for spiritual and recreational purposes.

These divergent and incommensurable practices tend to produce conflicts between different modes of organising on the land. Such conflicts do not just emerge because of different "stakeholder" values and interests, but because of the ontological differences stemming from incommensurable ways of relating to Earth itself. For example, from within Indigenous relational ontologies (see Chapter 4), a river, a mountain, or a forest is not just a site abundant in natural resources that can be exploited, developed, or protected by humans, but considered as a living being with its own will and agency (de la Cadena, 2015).

In instances when "different worlds collide" responsible organising needs to account for how the politics of this ontological multiplicity impacts what is considered "sustainable" and "responsible" by the different actors involved. Drawing on a Political Ontology (PO) frame

DOI: 10.4324/9781003229728-24

of analysis, and examples from Sámi homelands in Finland and the Mapuche territories in Chile, we discuss the politics of responsible organising in encounters between corporate and local Indigenous worlds. We seek to answer the question of what it means to act responsibly in contexts of ontological multiplicity.

Recognising ontological multiplicity

In PO, ontology refers to three interlinked understandings (Blaser 2010). First, ontology refers to the classical definition of the implicit and explicit assumptions a social group makes about their reality or the kinds of beings that exist and the conditions of their existence. Second, ontologies are understood to be performative; they perform themselves into being through the practices that connect people with land, waters, and other nonhuman beings in particular ways. The analytical concern is to understand how the performances of specific practices ("worldings") bring different worlds/ontologies into being. The use of the term "worlding" refers to the performative effects that particular practices have on the world that is being created. Hence, the world is not a singular unit "out there," of which people make sense based on different cultural values or beliefs. Rather, different ontologically dependent practices perform particular "worlds" into being, by connecting people, things, and other living beings in particular ways. Third, ontologies manifest through stories that make the assumptions of a given world "graspable," while also shaped by the realities they narrate. (Blaser, 2010)

PO scholars pay attention to the politics "between worlds," or how the dominant modern ontology through its ontological assumptions and performances (narrated through "the modern myth") excludes and ignores the existence of other ways of worlding, that is, ontological multiplicity (Blaser, 2010; de la Cadena, 2015). To make visible the ontological multiplicity stemming from nonmodern practices, PO scholars refer to the concept of "the pluriverse," as the unfolding of many overlapping ways of worlding that do not possess any overarching universal principle that unites the multiplicity (Blaser, 2010).

The dominance of the modern ontology is what enables the singularisation and occlusion of the pluriverse and its multiple worlding practices. In particular, the modern assumption of dualism separates between subjects and objects (or people and nature; see Chapter 17) and enables the use of scientific enquiries that create universally applicable facts about the world "out there," while relegating other ways of locally embedded and contextualised knowledge practices as "cultural beliefs" (Blaser, 2010). Also, the modern ontology's (uni)linear conception of time constructs a reality that assumes that the rest of the world will follow Europe's progress towards material prosperity and globalisation, portraying modern ways of being as advanced and superior, while others are backward and inferior (Blaser, 2010; Escobar, 2008). Yet, this depiction of history fails to account for how European material prosperity is built on colonial violence and enslavement of peoples and natures (Escobar, 2008). Through racial and gender hierarchies, the modern ontology occludes the negative effects it produces on other worlding practices while naturalising the modern world's ontological assumptions as the only one (Blaser, 2010). Through these assumptions, the modern ontology performs itself into existence as "the world," subjecting all other ways of worlding to its terms or considering them non-existent (Escobar 2008).

Challenging the superiority of the modern ontology

Recognising the ontological multiplicity of the pluriverse challenges the superiority of the modern ontology and makes visible other ways of relating to the world. Here we discuss two examples where the superiority of the modern ontology is challenged based on experiences from Sámi homelands in Finland and Mapuche territories in Chile. These show how ontological politics play out differently in contexts marked by colonialism. The Sámis have enjoyed a certain degree of inclusion in the Finnish regulatory institution and have a degree of self-determination through the Sámi parliament. They still have a deep connection to their ancestral homelands, although this connection is endangered. They engage in the defence of their threatened worlds, defending their views of what it means to be sustainable on the land. For the Mapuche, who have faced a much harsher exclusion, the organising efforts in defence of life are also about reclaiming and restoring lost worlds.

Sápmi: ontological contestations over sustainability

Sápmi, the Sámi homelands, comprises parts of northern Finland, Sweden, and Norway, and the Russian Kola Peninsula. The Sámi population is estimated at 80,000–100,000 with approximately 10,000 in Finland. In the Sámi context, settler colonialism reflects the continuity of the colonial structure of the state-led occupation of Sámi lands since the 17th century that continues to this date. According to the Sámi, the expansion of settler colonialism in Sápmi has led to a gradual increase in the use of natural resources, exceeding what these fragile lands can sustain. Today, Sápmi marks the borderland where the decolonising processes of the Sámi people confront the expansion of novel development projects, pushed in the name of sustainable development by the Finnish state and companies.

National and international regulations on Indigenous peoples' rights (e.g., the Finnish Constitution, the Sámi Parliament Act, Akwé: Kon guidelines on biodiversity on Indigenous lands) provide the Sámi with institutional protection in the planning of development projects (e.g., mining, tourism, infrastructure, wind power) on their lands. Yet, these projects still pose constant threats to the Sámi way of life. An example of such a project is the "Arctic Railway," proposed to stretch 500 kilometres from Finland's existing rail network in Rovaniemi to Kirkenes, a Norwegian port on the Barents Sea. The Sámi concern is that this project would split and fragment the Sámi homelands, with serious consequences for reindeer herding and other land-related practices (Jääskeläinen, 2021).

National and regional economic development agencies and investing companies justify projects by claiming they contribute to Arctic sustainable development and provide metals needed for the green economy transition (Tiainen et al., 2015). To comply with public and investor expectations of responsibility, corporations and governmental actors have produced numerous reports and indicators on land use planning, environmental and human rights impact assessments, corporate social responsibility (CSR) practices, and stakeholder engagements. For example, Finest Bay Area Development Ltd., the company in charge of the Arctic Railway, produces artificial intelligence technology to measure the progress of its development projects, referring to those numbers as "facts" about how its projects contribute to the United Nations Sustainable Development Goals (SDGs) (see Finest Bay Area Development, n.d.). Such measuring practices prioritise economic and work-related dimensions of sustainable development while using calculations about climate emissions selectively, separating the measurements from the contextual settings impacted (e.g., SDGs 10, 11, 13, and 15).

However, for the Sámi people, sustainability is not about who has the power to define sustainability in assessment reports or about measures of a separate nature "out there." Sustainability is a question of what kind of consequences these projects will have on the continuation of their worlding practices and ways of life. Sámi land-based practices involve a deep sense of reciprocity and responsibility towards the lands that protects and maintains the survival and well-being of the people, not abiding by growth imperatives set by the Finnish state. In deliberations with corporate and state representatives on the impact of the planned investments, Sámi notions of what it means to be sustainable on the land are often ignored. A common argument is that reindeer herding practices are "in need of modernisation," or that they are not "Indigenous anymore" (Jääskeläinen, 2021). Thus, the contemporary Sámi way of life is evaluated based on a linear conception of history and disregarded as either too "advanced" or "backward" to be considered truly "Indigenous." This is an example of how ontological multiplicity is erased. In response to development projects, the Sámi are forced to engage in a continuous defence of their lived-in worlds.

Chile: the resurgence of alternative worlds in Wallmapu

The expansion of the forestry industry in southern Chile follows a long trajectory wherein the Mapuche Indigenous people have suffered from colonialism and state violence in their homelands. During the Chilean dictatorship (1973–1990) vast areas of public land and forestry companies previously owned by the state were auctioned out to private companies. The implementation of a new forestry law in 1974 (Decree 701) offered subsidies of up to 75 per cent of the costs of tree plantations on lands regarded as suitable for forestry – this led to the rapid expansion of non-native, monoculture tree plantations (pine and eucalyptus) on lands that historically belonged to the Mapuche. Today, forestry plantations owned by companies cover almost three million hectares, while Mapuche communities live on less than 300,000 hectares. Prior to the Chilean colonisation in 1883, the Mapuche enjoyed autonomy over 10 million hectares of land, of which at the turn of century 40 per cent had been handed over to Chilean and European settlers (Pairican, 2014).

Due to the implementation of the forestry model, Mapuche communities have further suffered from land dispossessions, economic marginalisation, and environmental degradation. The tree plantations and the forestry extractive practices have serious impact on everyday lives (e.g., water scarcity, increased pollution), which has weakened the Mapuche ways of worlding (weakening the performances of SDGs 10, 13, 15). Locals report that the "*ngen*" – or the forces, energies, and spirits living in the life-sustaining webs of relations in Mapuche territories – have disappeared due to the tree plantations (González Correa, 2019).

Since the late 1990s, Mapuche groups have actively mobilised against the forestry companies, reclaiming their stolen lands (Pairican, 2014). The state has responded in vigour, criminalising community members and militarising the Mapuche territories (Pairican, 2014). While the more violent features of the Mapuche struggle are contained by Chilean police forces, companies have invested in elaborate CSR practices aimed at creating a "shared value" with the communities where they operate. Such strategic interventions in the community both obfuscate the Mapuche's claim for autonomy and self-determination and occlude the Mapuche processes of decolonisation, where local communities reclaim their ancestral ways of worlding and relating to land.

These visible confrontations embody a deeper ontological conflict about what land is, and how to live with land (Ehrnström-Fuentes, 2020; González Correa, 2019). Many Mapuche movements are not just focused on reclaiming (ownership of) their lost territories, they also actively work on generating alternatives based on their ancestral worlding practices (Ehrnström-Fuentes, 2020; González Correa, 2019). Through practices that restore balance on the land, such as increasing self-sufficiency of food, replacing pine and eucalyptus with native trees, protecting springs, and taking care of water, these movements defend and promote the "*iltrofill mongen*" (respect for everything that lives) (González Correa, 2019, p. 105). These restoration practices are an example of how local movements challenge extractive corporate practices on their land by bringing alternative worlds that do not separate people and nature into being (Ehrnström-Fuentes, 2020).

Conclusion

This chapter has addressed the question of what it means to act responsibly in contexts of ontological multiplicity and land-based conflicts. The Sámi and Mapuche experiences of conflictive encounters with extractive ways of relating to the land show that different worlding practices create different and at time conflictive responsibilities and sustainabilities. Responsible organising in these contexts of ontological multiplicity is political; how people and organisations connect to the nonhuman world through either extractive or restorative relations has implications for what kind of responsibilities and sustainabilities are brought into being.

The modern ontology, performed through practices that separate between people and nature, is challenged by local movements that organise to defend their own ways of worlding. These contestations make visible the politics at play when the ontological multiplicity of the pluriverse manifests itself and challenges what the modern ontology define as real. To grasp the ontological politics of responsible organising we need to pay attention to the deeper ontological issues at stake when people mobilise to defend and reclaim their ways of worlding.

140   *Maria Ehrnström-Fuentes and Tiina Jääskeläinen*

References

Blaser, M. (2010). *Storytelling Globalization from the Chaco and Beyond.* Duke University Press.
De la Cadena, M. (2015). *Earth-Beings: Ecologies of Practice across Andean Worlds.* Duke University Press.
Ehrnström-Fuentes, M. (2020). Organising in defence of life: The emergence and dynamics of a territorial movement in Southern Chile. *Organization.* October. https://doi.org/110.1177/1350508420963871
Escobar, A. (2008). *Territories of Difference: Place, Movements, Life, Redes.* Duke University Press.
Finest Bay Area Development (n.d.). Sustainable Development Goals Scorecard. Available from https://finestbayarea.online/media/89
González Correa, V.G. (2019). *Resistencia de mujeres lavkenche al modelo forestal de Chile,* Master's Thesis at CIESA, Mexico.
Jääskeläinen, T. (2021). Invalidation techniques, group-related epistemic differences and practices of exclusion during sustainability crisis – A case study about recognition for Sámi ways of life in the reassembling of the Arctic, Conference Proceeding, EGOS 2021.
Pairican, F. (2014). *Malon: La Rebelión del Movimiento Mapuche 1990–2013.* Santiago de Chile: Pehuén Editores.
Tiainen, H., Sairinen, R., & Sidorenko, O. (2015). Governance of Sustainable Mining in Arctic Countries: Finland, Sweden, Greenland & Russia. In: L. Heininen , H. Exner-Pirot, & J. Plouffe. (eds.). *Arctic Yearbook 2015.* Akureyri: Northern Research Forum. Available from www.arcticyearbook.com.

Part V

Responsible organising

Ways forward

21 Responsible organising

Ways forward

Maria Sandberg and Janne Tienari

Introduction

The chapters in this interdisciplinary book have critically examined sustainability challenges that humankind faces and suggested responsible ways of organising as a solution in responding to these challenges. The authors have offered a multitude of ways that different actors can organise for transformative action towards sustainable outcomes, as expressed in the United Nations Sustainable Development Goals (SDGs). The point of departure of the book was that urgent action is needed in and across organisations and societies. The need for change and transformation is reflected in all chapters, which address different SDGs, discuss different challenges, and propose different solutions. This final chapter brings these discussions together to suggest ways forward for responsible organising.

We begin by reviewing what the chapters tell us about how we can respond to the SDGs. The chapters offer examples and discussions of how different actors can work to achieve the SDGs, but also of how the SDGs must be challenged and developed so that they even better reflect the complex and interconnected sustainability challenges that we are facing.

Next, we offer some concluding remarks on the two main concepts of the book: "responsible" and "organising." We discuss how the authors suggest to (re)define the meaning of responsibility when organising for sustainable outcomes. We then summarise the different forms of transformative action they suggest moving forward, captured under two themes: transcending business and rediscovering politics.

Sustainable outcomes: towards and beyond the SDGs

The book has examined how we can work to achieve sustainable outcomes, as expressed in the SDGs. The chapters have covered a wide

DOI: 10.4324/9781003229728-26

variety of both social and environmental sustainability challenges. Social issues covered include, among others, reducing poverty (SDG 1; in e.g., Chapter 13), access to clean water (SDG 6; in Chapter 18), and achieving gender equality (SDG 5; in Chapters 15 and 16). Environmental challenges covered in the book include, among others, clean energy transitions (SDG 7; in Chapter 8) and sustainable resource use (SDG 15; in Chapter 10).

The book chapters have suggested a variety of ways to achieve different SDGs. These include legislation (Chapters 7 and 10), companies' business model innovations and marketing (Chapter 11), mobilisation (Chapter 2) and operations of non-governmental organisations (NGOs; Chapter 10), and local communities (Chapters 4, 17, and 20). A particular focus has been the potential of partnerships between actors (SDG 17). The chapters have discussed an ecosystem approach to responsible organising (Chapter 8) as well as multi-stakeholder, cross-sector collaborations (Chapters 7 and 13). The SDGs have been suggested as a potential platform around which to globally organise for transformative action towards sustainable outcomes (Chapters 5 and 6).

It is important to recognise the interconnectedness of the SDGs. Achieving sustainable outcomes often involves complex interplay and potential conflicts between different SDGs. Most chapters in the book address more than one of the SDGs. Chapter 5, in particular, brings links between various SDGs to the forefront, discussing how global pandemics have effects not only on health (SDG 3), but also on, for example, education (SDG 4) and inequality (SDG 10). Similarly, Chapter 9 illustrates how a focus on fostering innovation (SDG 9) can endanger the achievement of other goals, such as health and well-being (SDG 3) and decent work (SDG 8).

However, the book also recognises that the SDGs need to be critically examined and further developed for action towards sustainable outcomes to become truly transformative. In particular, many chapters are critical of the human-centric approach to environmental challenges that dominates the SDGs (SDGs 13, 14, and 15). Several of the chapters discuss how to overcome the nature–human dichotomy central to modern thinking (Chapter 17), suggesting a need for relational and reciprocal engagements with the nonhuman world (Chapter 4) that includes nonhuman animals (Chapter 19) as well as other non-human entities. Respecting and learning from the nature relations of local, Indigenous communities is strongly present in these discussions (Chapters 4, 17, and 20).

The book also critically addresses current ways of attempting to reduce inequalities (SDGs 5 and 10). Chapters examine humanitarian relief (Chapter 12), multi-stakeholder partnerships (Chapter 13), social media (Chapter 14), and working conditions in both the Global South (Chapter 15) and the Global North (Chapter 16). The book is critical of the concept of diversity (Chapter 3) and suggests intersectional analyses to overcome some of its shortcomings (Chapters 15 and 16). In addition, chapters argue that many current efforts for sustainability fail to address structural inequalities between the Global North and the Global South (Chapters 12 and 13).

In addition, the book critically examines the failure of corporate social responsibility (CSR) to address sustainability (Chapter 2), problematises the notion of "affordable" water (SDG 6; in Chapter 18), and highlights the potential irresponsibility of innovations (SDG 9; in Chapter 9). Chapter 6 suggests the SDGs as a potential platform to discuss and reconcile different interpretations of sustainability and responsibility. We conclude that transformative action for sustainable outcomes requires not only responsibly organising for the SDGs as presently formulated and interpreted but going beyond these formulations and interpretations to critically examine whether the SDGs are sufficient for transformative action.

What is responsible?

A key concept in the book is responsibility. Transformative action for sustainable outcomes requires a reflexive understanding and analysis of what "responsible" organising entails. We call for more critical perspectives in research on responsibility, (in)equality, and sustainability. The chapters provide many examples of how we can critically examine and (re)define what responsibility means when organising for sustainable outcomes.

Several chapters in the book take a notably critical approach to companies and the hegemony of market-based logics in tackling sustainability challenges, in particular social inequalities. Chapter 12, for example, offers a critical take on what the authors call logistification of humanitarian relief. When operationalised in crisis situations in the Global South, relief initiatives take problematic forms and can have detrimental consequences for local populations. According to the authors, there is an urgent need to rethink how relief and its supply chains are organised. "Corporate saviourism" in the Global South is critically scrutinised in Chapter 13, where the authors show how acts of goodwill by companies and market-based NGOs aim to install ideas of entrepreneurship and individualised responsibility into societies with very different traditions. For multi-stakeholder partnerships to become truly transformative, the authors argue that people in local communities as well as what the authors call "inclusive" governments must become part of them as power holders.

In both examples, current ways of organising are upholding a capitalist social order and unequal relations between the Global North and Global South. Similarly, Chapter 18 highlights problems related to market-based solutions to accessing water in the Global South. The authors argue that turning water into a privatisation-compatible project and a question of affordability rather than human right can have disastrous consequences for local communities and people. They point to social inequalities resulting from private companies' efforts to govern, control, and manage water.

Further, the well-being of people in challenging conditions of work and life is highlighted in several chapters, whether calling for contextually sensitive understandings of intersectionality (Chapter 15) or for valuing care and seeing work and care as intertwined rather than as separate domains, where care can be downplayed or even ignored in work organisations (Chapter 16). Companies are advised to take their responsibility over social equality seriously. This spills over to online spaces such as social media where social injustice, exclusion, and discrimination are reinforced (Chapter 14).

In addition, many authors in the book present a case for challenging human-centric views in discussions of sustainability. Echoing the agenda set in Chapter 4, authors argue for extending the notion of responsibility beyond humans to include the natural environment and nonhuman animals. Chapter 17 shows how the nature–human dichotomy is defied by local realities and understandings. Chapter 19 with its focus on animal welfare argues that sustainable development should be an interspecies agenda. The authors highlight an issue that is taken up in many chapters: human and nonhuman well-being are interconnected. Taking care of people is not enough. Visions, strategies, and management of companies and other organisations must recognise this. Finally, Chapter 20 turns our attention to different ontological assumptions about "the world" that influence what kind of organising activities and relations to nonhumans are considered responsible and sustainable. The authors show how and why these assumptions matter in making sense of the politics of responsible organising.

Organising: transcending business, rediscovering politics

The book is critical of currently dominating ways to organise for sustainable outcomes, characterised by an (over)emphasis on market-based and corporate solutions and exemplified by concepts such as CSR (Chapter 2), diversity (Chapter 3), and innovation (Chapter 9). The book suggests a need to transcend this business-centred approach as humankind seeks to find solutions to tackle sustainability challenges. Many chapters explicitly or implicitly argue that ways forward include rediscovering politics. This entails political actors and institutions at all levels taking a more central role in tackling sustainability challenges.

We argue that market-based solutions alone do not suffice, and that politics must reconquer some of the spaces it has lost to private business. Transformative political action is needed at all levels: local, national, and transnational. By political actors we refer to transnational institutions such as the United Nations and the European Union, to states and governments, and, crucially, to local communities and civil society actors such as NGOs and their ways of organising and exerting political influence. Some of the ideas presented in the chapters serve to complement market-driven solutions, while others operate as alternatives for them.

Chapters 5 and 6 set the scene for rediscovering politics in the contemporary world. Chapter 5 brings to the fore the political nature of many global and systemic risks. Political actors and institutions are elementary in preparing for these risks and in dealing with their consequences. The COVID-19 pandemic is discussed as an example of this. Chapter 6 highlights the return of global geopolitics and uses the example of China versus USA in elucidating how politics of powerful nation-states intertwine with, for example, development of technology. The authors envision a role for transnational political institutions such as the United Nations in the era of geopolitics.

In line with Chapter 2, political pressure is needed on companies in many industries to move their thinking and actions towards responsibility. Chapter 7 highlights how political action can provide a means for diverse actors, including companies, to collectively push for regulating how companies can do good and avoid doing harm. Operating on the societal level, this chapter shows how collective political action that aims at regulating corporate conduct is possible. Chapter 10 provides an example of how the EU as a political actor can through legislation steer how actors organise for sustainable outcomes. With the example of textile recycling and reuse, the authors discuss how new EU legislation is likely to change supply chains for post-use textiles.

While companies in many industries are spear-heading action for sustainable outcomes, the ideas and solutions offered in this book transcend the boundaries of individual organisations and their business interests. Transformative action for sustainable outcomes requires collaborative efforts between a multitude of actors, ranging from local communities to companies and other organisations to transnational networks.

Many of the authors emphasise new forms of multi-stakeholder collaboration between companies and political actors such as non-governmental and non-profit organisations and labour unions. For example, the authors of Chapter 2 highlight the role of stakeholders such as NGOs in changing the behaviour of companies. The ecosystem approach foregrounded in Chapter 8, too, has a political dimension as among the key actors in the studied regionally based ecosystem is a public sector entity: a local city. The authors argue for collaboration between different actors in finding "win-win-win" solutions where they can all benefit. In challenging the traditional logic of markets and marketing, in turn, Chapter 11 illustrates how both individual advocates (such as social media influencers) and established institutions (such as political decision-makers and the state) can leverage new channels to transmit critical information regarding the environment and society and influence purposeful collective action towards sustainable outcomes.

Conclusion

This edited book comprising 21 chapters brings together discussions on how we can organise responsibly for transformative action towards sustainable outcomes, as expressed in the United Nations SDGs. The book critically examines current ways of organising and provides a plethora of examples of ways forward. We hope that it inspires practitioners in efforts to achieve the SDGs and researchers and students in future research on responsible organising, and that it engenders meaningful collaboration between practitioners and academics. This final chapter has provided suggestions for ways forward that we hope can serve as a starting point for future efforts to tackle social inequalities, environmental degradation, and other sustainability challenges.

The chapters in the book emphasise a reflexive understanding of what actions are "responsible" and why when organising for sustainable outcomes. The authors also point to a need to transcend business and corporate activities in addressing sustainability challenges. The book argues that politics must be rediscovered as part of the solution if humankind is to survive and prosper. On the one hand, the need for transnational politics is highlighted. On the other, the importance of local initiatives and movements is recognised. Overall, actions and activities must transcend the boundaries of individual organisations into new forms of collaborative – or agonistic – multi-stakeholder relationships, networks, and ecosystems and go beyond human-centric understandings of responsibility, equality, and sustainability.

This means that we as practitioners and researchers balance between different views and interests and are open to challenging conventional ways of thinking. We see responsible organising as a perspective that allows to bridge gaps between practitioners and researchers and offers an open-minded and forward-looking agenda for research and activism.

Index

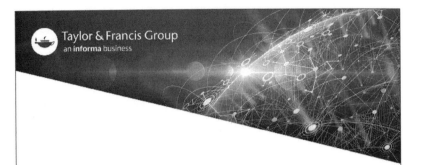

Printed and bound by CPI Group (UK) Ltd, Croydon, CR0 4YY

11/04/2025

01844010-0017